Maybe Tomorrow

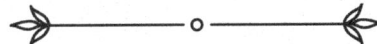

Patricia McCain

© Patricia McCain 2022

ISBN: 978-1-66787-143-1
eBook ISBN: 978-1-66787-144-8

All rights reserved. This book or any portion thereof may not be reproduced or used in any manner whatsoever without the express written permission of the publisher except for the use of brief quotations in a book review.

CONTENTS

Acknowledgements:

For all the encouragement and help I have received I give my thanks to my daughter and son in law Debbie and Darren Rice. I am so very grateful for their guidance along the way. I also want to thank Emily McCain for providing the beautiful picture for my cover. And, for making me want to proceed with getting my book to a publisher, I want to also thank my friend and neighbor Rachel Wines for reading what I had written and giving me her encouragement. Most of all I need to thank my publisher BookBaby for making the final project one that I can truly be proud of. I have been guided along the way with the help of many prayers. I truly believe that God has been with me all along the way to keep on writing and to proceed. *Maybe Tomorrow* has been in the works for almost 10 years.

PART I: ADELLA

CHAPTER 1
Adella, 1920–1942

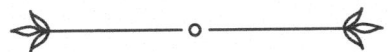

Okmulgee, Oklahoma

Adella loved Edward very much, from the first day they met. It had been a hard life, and she was determined to improve it.

Her father had died of pneumonia when she was only five years old, and she had no memory of him other than that he was never there. Adella was one of five children. The year was 1920.

Life was hard for everyone, including her mother, who was suddenly left alone to take care of herself and all her children. They survived off of water biscuits and water gravy that her mother prepared. At times, the close neighbors would pick fresh vegetables from their gardens and bring them to Adella's mother. That was always a feast for her family.

As she grew older, Adella realized the best thing she could do would be to find work to help ease the burden on her mother and improve her own life. She was not content to live that type of life in such a small community. So, at sixteen, Adella decided to move out and be on her own.

She found a ride from a friend, took one small bag of personal belongings, then moved herself to the big city of Tulsa, Oklahoma. She had some friends who lived there, so she quickly arranged to stay with them.

She found a carhop job close to where they lived and could walk back and forth to work. That job lasted almost one year and was just on the outskirts of town. She sent what she could home to her mom. At the same time, she was saving what she could to pay for the training she wanted more than anything—training to become a nurse. The tips she received from some of her customers were more significant than her salary, which helped her savings grow even faster.

One night, a wealthy and very drunk customer was delighted with her, so he gave her a tip of one hundred dollars. She tried to return it to him, but he would not accept it. Going home that night, she was feeling pretty happy. She decided that she would move to a better part of town and get a better job. It was time to move up in the world.

Adella was not content to stay in one place all her life like her brothers and sister had decided to do. She took her time choosing the best location to meet influential people. Adella wanted a place to better herself but didn't have the training to get a perfect job. She did have the determination and inner strength to know she could do anything.

At the Crown Drug Store in the central part of Tulsa's downtown business world, Adella noticed how frequently business people went there for lunch. She also saw the sign in the window, "Fountain Help Wanted!"

She bought herself a lovely dress, hose, and smart-looking shoes with a small amount of money she had set aside. She wanted to look sharp. She was worried that she might not be able to buy enough clothes to wear if she got the job. But she told herself she would cross that bridge when she came to it. She didn't doubt that she would get the job, and her determination proved justified when Mr. Clark, the manager, decided to hire her.

That night, as she was preparing to move into a small furnished apartment closer to her job, she felt pretty proud of herself. She was eighteen years old and had managed to get the job, move to a more excellent place, and put 175 dollars in the bank for her future nurse's training. When Mr. Clark, her new boss, told her that she would be supplied uniforms for the job as a fountain clerk, it was the frosting on the cake, especially since they were nice, clean, white uniforms similar to that of a nurse's uniform.

After just a few years of working, Adella had begun to enjoy the friendships she was making with the regular lunch crowd, and her nest egg was slowly building up toward her nurse's training.

Then one day a man walked up to the counter, took a seat on the stool, removed his hat, re-lit his pipe, and smiled at her.

"Hi. Will you go out with me tonight for dinner?" he asked.

She had never seen him before. He was not a usual customer. When he had first entered the drug store, their eyes had met, and from then on, no one else existed for her.

He was the most handsome man she had ever noticed. He was very tall, dressed like a million bucks, and held that pipe in his hands as though it were a part of him. His self-assurance left no doubt in her mind that this was someone exceptional. So it seemed only fitting to her to say, "Yes, I will have dinner with you tonight!"

Dating was new to her. She had never thought of doing anything like this before. Dating or even loving someone had never been in her plans for her future. There was no time for a man or love as far as she was concerned.

On May 6, 1937, they were married—less than a week after meeting each other. He swept her off her feet. He was Edward Bevins, the son of Mr. and Mrs. Bevins, who owned the drugstore she worked for and some of the other big dairy stores in Tulsa. Edward's parents had always given their son whatever he wanted, and if he had decided he wanted Adella, they would sign the consent for him to get married. Adella didn't know what had hit her. She only knew that she worshipped him and would do anything he asked of her.

It took less than a month for her to discover that Edward was only seventeen years old, spoiled rotten, and gave no thought to the future. Edward's way of having fun was to gamble with the money his parents supplied for him and party at any chance he found. A solid job was the last thing he ever wanted.

"Don't worry, Adella," he would tell her. "We have all the money we need. Mom and Dad will take care of whatever we want."

CHAPTER 2

Tulsa: Married Life, 1937

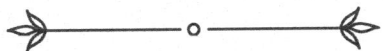

Edward's parents were happy, and they did take care of them. They felt a wife would suit Edward and help him grow up. When they met Adella, they immediately liked her. She was older than him, and they'd heard she wanted to become a nurse. She seemed very responsible and appeared to have a strong head on her shoulders. Responsibility was something that Edward Jr. had never had. On their wedding day, Edward's parents told Adella that they wanted to help them in every way they could, and they did just that.

They bought them a car, put a nice amount of money in Jr.'s bank account, and paid for an apartment. They did what they could to make life easy for the newly married couple.

Edward was perfectly content just living off his parents' money and having a wife to support him and take care of him, as he thought a wife should.

Adella was happy, as she idolized him. She loved waiting on him hand and foot, and she loved having to care for him. But she was also very accustomed to taking care of herself.

Adella insisted on keeping her job and didn't like him trying to change her. Nursing was still on her mind, but Edward would not hear of it, so she did not force the issue. She just continued saving what money she could and kept it hidden from him, knowing that someday she would fulfill her dream of being a nurse.

One year after Edward and Adella were married, Mr. Belvins became ill and died suddenly in a fire, leaving the bulk of his estate and the dairy businesses he owned to Edward. It was only one month after that when Mrs. Belvins committed suicide. Life without her husband was more than she could bear.

It didn't take long for Edward to sell all the dairy businesses his family had given him and his parents' home for less than one-third of what it was worth to one of his gambling buddies. He would have given it to his buddy if he had asked for it because he didn't want all that responsibility, and he was too young and foolish to care. Edward did not discuss any of this with Adella. He just did it and would later tell her what he had done.

Adella soon discovered that she was pregnant. She had not planned to have a child this soon but was happy. Adella was carrying the child of the man she loved so profoundly. She told him she was pregnant late one night after he had made love to her.

"Honey, we are going to be parents. It's time for you to settle down and find a job," Adella told him.

Edward loved her in his way, but he was not ready to become a father and was not willing to settle down.

He fraudulently put down his age as twenty-one and joined the United States Army the next day. It was now 1938, and he was packed and ready to go in two hours. Finally, he told her what he had done.

"You can use the money left to help with the baby's expenses. Then send some to your mother so she can come and be with you. If we have a girl, name her Lori Ann. We can call her Lori for short. She can be my little princess." he said.

He hugged and kissed her, and he was gone!

Adella worked as long as she could and saved as much money as possible, knowing she would soon have to send for her mother. She would need to have someone live with her after her baby was born. Her baby was a girl, and Adella did what her husband Edward asked her to do. She named their daughter Lori Ann.

Edward managed to get a temporary leave to come home for the birth of his first child. Adella watched him as he carefully took Lori Ann in his arms. Her love for Edward was as strong as it had been that first day he had entered the Crown Drug Store. He had on his Army uniform, and to her, he was even more handsome than before.

The tears ran from her eyes as she watched him holding their new baby daughter. She watched as he gingerly kissed her on the forehead and said, "I christen you Princess, my princess."

He was only home for a few days' leave, and before Adella knew it, she was alone again.

Adella's mother, Jane, had come to stay with her for the birth of her baby. She told Adella what she thought she needed to do.

"You need to come back home with me to Okmulgee. I can take care of Lori, and you can use the money you have saved to start your training as a nurse at our local hospital. Edward is gone now, and it may be four years before he will be out of the Army. Use this time to do what you have always wanted to do," she said.

Adella knew her mother was right. She was getting nowhere the way things were now. She also knew that not just anybody would take proper care of her baby. She still felt full of ambition and the desire to become a nurse. There was no question in her mind about what she had to do.

She moved back to Okmulgee in August of 1938 with her mother, enrolled in nurse's training, and started her new future with Dr. T.R. Cook, the local hospital's owner. He immediately liked Adella and took her under his wing to supervise her training.

"On-the-job training is better than any amount of schooling you can get," he told her.

In the evenings after her school training, she worked side by side with him at the hospital. Dr. Cook was a petite man with a twinkle in his eyes that made her feel content and comfortable just being around him. She found the more she learned from him, the more she wanted to learn. She knew she had found her destiny.

During her training to become a licensed practical nurse, or LPN, Adella enjoyed her daughter when she could and worked with Dr. Cook in the evenings. She slowly built her savings account up again. But she still missed and wanted Edward back home with her.

Adella would read the letters she received from Edward repeatedly. She was marking the days off the calendar, waiting for his return home. By then, she would be an LPN, earning a good salary, and could give him the money she had saved so he could start his own business.

She knew Edward knew enough about the dairy business to start one of his own in Okmulgee. The town needed one badly. A college was nearby, and she knew the dairy alone would bring in many customers. She loved him very much and felt that after his years in the service, he would be mature enough to take on a new responsibility and make things work out so they could be happy together and start their lives over.

CHAPTER 3

Edward Returns Home, 1942

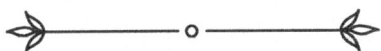

When the day finally came, Edward walked down the ramp, picked Adella up in his arms, and swung her around, kissing her on the lips, cheeks, and eyes.

As he carried her off the airplane ramp and to their car, she told him, "You are still sweeping me off my feet."

Every time Adella saw Edward, she fell in love with him all over again. He had matured in his looks and, hopefully, she was thinking, in his mind as she drove them to the home she had prepared for him.

Edward was delighted with Adella's new job as an LPN, and he was pleased with the home she had carefully prepared for him. He was also happy with his daughter, Lori, now almost four years old, who was pretty as a princess. He was pleased with the money she handed him as a welcome home gift.

"You are quite a woman," he told her.

As they lay in bed, Adella spoke to him softly, saying, "Please promise me that you will use the money I gave you to start yourself a dairy business here so we can settle down and become a family."

"Okay, sweetheart, if it will make you happy. I will settle down and act like an old married man. Now hush, and come here so we can make Lori a little brother," he replied.

The years she had struggled without him were now in the past. She now had him home, and Edward filled her with happiness. Peaceful, restful sleep came easy for her that night.

The note she found on the kitchen table that following day read: "I thought I would drive to Tulsa and look up some of my old buddies. Take care. I will be home in a few days. Love, Edward."

Two weeks later, he drove up in the driveway. Adella was in the kitchen trying to stay busy, worried sick about him. He had called her once and smoothed things out, telling her he would be home Sunday. She had already forgiven him, realizing that he did need some time for himself before he had to settle down. She had decided to fix a nice meal and make him feel glad to be back home.

The cornbread was ready to pop in the oven. Adella had just turned the fire off the big pot of beans she had prepared, fixing them just the way he liked, when she noticed a car pulling into the driveway. She realized it was Edward, but it was not her car—the car that she had bought.

Edward tried to explain what he had done as he quickly entered the house and headed straight to the bathroom. He called to her as he sat on the toilet, "I did trade in your car because I was not too fond of it."

"But Edward, that one was paid for," she yelled back at him from the kitchen, trying to compose herself.

"Don't worry about it, honey," he yelled back at her. "The payments are not much, and we can handle them."

"Edward, please tell me you did not use some of the money I gave you on the car. That money was to open your new business," she said.

She picked up the beans and walked to the bathroom door to wait for his answer. She stood there looking down at him, waiting, but no answer came. He sat there looking down into the water in the space between his legs.

"There isn't any of the money left," he said.

"What do you mean there isn't any left?" she asked him quietly.

"I lost it all gambling with my buddies," he answered without even looking up.

It was an instant reflex that made Adella do what she did. The pot of beans now became a part of Edward. She dumped the bowl on top of his head. Beans ran over his face, chest, and down into the space between his legs. He suddenly was not near as handsome as she remembered.

The only thing she hated now was that she had walls and the floor to clean up. Edward could worry about himself! She damn sure was not going to anymore.

Edward was not going to worry about himself anymore either. He found it easier to let Uncle Sam take care of him, so he re-enlisted and joined the Navy the next day. To him, life was taking each day as it came, doing what felt good to him at the time. The future would take care of itself. Edward had too much fun and didn't want to care for a family or a business. Adella's dreams were just too high.

He knew she loved him and would be there for him whenever he returned, no matter what. At a very young age, he decided to take whatever life could offer him and not worry about the consequences.

Edward spent time in the Navy and was able to come home twice. While Edward was serving his country one more time, Adella gave birth to a baby boy, and they named him Terrell.

PART II: LORI

CHAPTER 4

Okmulgee: Lori, Age 5, 1943

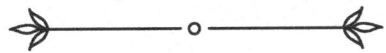

When my mom, Adella, moved us in with her mother, Jane, I was five. It was a tiny house built for Jane by her son-in-law, my uncle Chuck. The house was on the same property as his. I remember we were all just in one big room with two beds. I knew Mom was doing her best since Dad had to be gone. I remember that Jane, my granny, always read stories to Terrell and me from the Bible at bedtime. I did enjoy what she would read to us, even if I didn't understand it. I just loved the peacefulness of her voice, and I knew it would help me go to sleep.

My first real memory of hope and fear came when I entered the first grade. We were still living with Granny while Mom was working at the hospital. One day, Mom was late picking me up from school. She had told me to sit on the steps to wait for her, and it would always feel good to see her car pull up to the curb so I could run and jump in. Mom had also told me never to leave those steps or get into another vehicle with a stranger.

She had scared me bad enough, so I knew I would never leave those steps with anyone other than her. But that day, our school was out, and it was getting later and later. All my other friends had been picked up except Bruce, one of my classmates.

"My mom is late too, but I know she'll be here soon," he said.

I remember feeling a little frightened because it was getting so late. Bruce was sitting close beside me, but he somehow made me feel better.

"Do you think someone will try and grab us and put us in their car? I'm getting scared, Bruce. I wish Mom would hurry up and get here," I told him.

"Don't worry, I'll take care of you," he told me.

I remember the warmth of his arm around my shoulders, holding me tight against him, and how it had made me feel so much safer. It was a short time later when Mom pulled up to the curb. She got out of her car, walked over to where Bruce and I were sitting, then bent down and hugged us both.

"I'm so glad you stayed here together and waited for me. Bruce, your dad asked me to pick you up for him and bring you home," she told us.

Bruce knew it would be alright to go with my mom, but he asked her, "Why didn't my mom come after me?"

Mom then took both our hands and led us to her car.

"Bruce, your dad will explain that to you when you get home," Mom said.

Being safe in Mom's car felt good, but she seemed sad. As we pulled into Bruce's driveway, I noticed there were a lot of cars around.

"Lori, you stay right here in the car. I'll be right back," Mom told me.

She then took Bruce's hand and walked inside his house with him. After what seemed to be a very long time to me, she returned. I asked her why there were so many cars.

"Lori, Bruce's mother hasn't been well for a long time. Today she had a spell and didn't live through it. That's why I was so very late picking you up. I've been doing what I could to help his dad," she explained.

I didn't know what death meant, but it always saddened people. "Mom, Bruce made me feel safe when you were so late tonight. Does that mean I need to make him feel safe now?" I asked.

"Lori, any time you have a friend that needs you, in any way, you should always do what you can to make them feel better," she told me.

The next day at school, I remember waiting for Bruce to walk down the sidewalk to sit with me, but he never came. Bruce didn't return to school anymore. His dad moved them to another city. Bruce had touched my life one day, and then he was gone. But each day at school, I hoped he would show up again to sit beside me so I could try to make him feel like he had made me feel.

As far back as I can remember, as a young girl, the feeling of hope was always present. I learned that life was like a storybook at a very young age. Each month, each year would bring new pictures to your mind, new faces, and new stories to tell.

I used to walk in the open field behind Granny's little house whenever I had the chance. It was always the same field, but I hoped it would show me something different each day. And each day, it always would. There would be a new bloom on a flower, a new bird would fly by, or a baby rabbit would suddenly appear from nowhere.

These things, for a few moments, would always touch my life, then disappear. The breeze would either be hot or cool or maybe not even there. It might be sunny or cloudy. Each day I knew it was the same field, yet different. I always looked forward to my walks with Granny in that field or just walking it alone.

I also learned that if I hoped each day would bring me something new like in the storybooks Granny read, it would! She would tell me that maybe tomorrow we will see something we have not seen before.

Years later, as a grown woman, I could think back through each day, each year, and remember that life did bring me fear, hardships, doubt, sadness, and love. Life was just like everything in all those storybooks Granny used to read to me.

Most of all, life brought me hope. I know and believe a lot of this came from my granny and, most of all, my mom, Adella. I know I inherited their strength and determination.

CHAPTER 5

A Home of Our Own, 1944

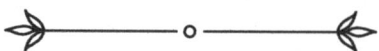

A few months later, Mom found us a house to move to that wasn't far from where Granny lived and was close to the city park. Somehow Mom managed to fill the house with furniture, dishes, and what we needed to make it feel like home. Terrell and I were so happy to have a bed and our own space.

It was during the years of World War Two, and everyone was doing what they could to keep their families and lives in some order. Dad managed to have a very short leave and could be home for a short time. When I first saw him in his Navy uniform, I thought he was the most handsome man I had ever seen. I had missed him so much, and I loved the feeling of his strength when he would kiss and hug me.

Mom was now a nurse, so she was also dressed in white. They both looked so very special to me. I think they guessed how I felt, so they bought me some white shorts, a white top, and a white sailor cap, just like Dad wore.

Mom and Dad took my brother Terrell and me to the park one day when he was home on leave. We had so much fun together playing ball and swimming. Dad told me that day that I would always be his princess, and if he stayed gone for a long time, just thinking of me as his princess would make time pass much faster for him.

That night as he tucked me into bed, I said, "I love you, Daddy, and I'm glad you are home. I hope you never have to leave us again."

"Goodnight, Princess," he said. "Be a good girl, and remember that I'll always love you."

The following day, Mom told me she would be gone for a few days.

"Daddy has to leave again to help fight the war. You and Terrell can stay with Granny until I get back," she said.

It was a very long time before Dad came back home again. A long time before I would feel his strong hugs—a long time before I would feel like a princess again.

A few years had passed, and Terrell and I would stay with Granny when Mom was at work. When I was there, I would spend a lot of time with my cousin Ellen. Ellen was Uncle Chuck and Aunt Sue's daughter. She was six months older than me and seemed smarter than everyone.

I noticed that the boys in her neighborhood seemed to pay more attention to her than they did to me, so I was always jealous of her. I couldn't figure out why her dad was at home, and mine was off fighting a war. Ellen even had an older brother instead of a younger one. He didn't bother her at all. Not like Terrell did me. Her brother was always there to help her and take care of her.

I loved Uncle Chuck, Granny's son-in-law. He was always laughing or smiling and would make you smile too. He loved for you to come and sit on his knee, and then he would hug you and make you feel happy. Even though he was not my dad, he did make things better. I loved walking out to the pasture with him to help milk his cows or feed his chickens. It was fun to gather the eggs the chickens had laid.

Mom was working a lot at the hospital, so I spent a lot of time with Ellen, climbing up in the Apple Trees in the Orchard. I also found that it was a perfect place to hide from Terrell, and sometimes I would try to hide from Ellen. A lot of times, I just wanted to be alone.

I was so envious of Ellen! I was much taller than most boys my age, and she was short and petite. Her chest was developing, and mine was still flat. Most boys always wanted to hang around with her, not me. I would climb up to the highest branch in those apple trees to escape them all. I felt out of place and didn't belong when I was with them. I secretly hoped Uncle Chuck or Don, her brother, would walk by and see me. Maybe they would see how sad I looked, climb up there, put their arms around me, and hug me close. They could make me feel better like Bruce, my first real friend in school, had made me feel when I was in the first grade.

My granny was the one who always seemed to bring me happiness. When I stayed with her, I would crawl into bed and listen as she read from the Bible. I would ask her, "Granny, when will my dad come home?" Or, "Why is Ellen so big in her chest, and I'm not?" Or, "Why do I feel so good when Uncle Chuck hugs me?"

"Lori, there's an answer to all your questions right here in this Bible," she would tell me. "It would be best if you learned to read it. The Bible will help you to understand things as you grow up."

Then she would start reading again, and I would drift off to sleep, hoping I could learn all those big words. But most of all, hoping that I would understand all of them better.

One night as she was reading to me, I could not fall asleep. I noticed a red light blinking off and on just outside her window. Uncle Chuck had told me it was a radio tower, so I asked Granny, "Can the Bible tell me why that red light blinks off and on?"

After a few moments, she said, "Let me see what it says, Lori. It tells me that it's trying to help you go to sleep. Each time it blinks, it says to you, 'Lori, go to sleep. Lori, go to sleep. Lori, go to sleep.'"

As I watched it, my eyes grew heavier and heavier, and I would drift off to sleep. I thought to myself, that is the most thoughtful book I know. It has an answer to everything.

One day when I was staying with Granny while Mom was at work, the boys in the neighborhood and Ellen and I were messing around in the pasture behind Uncle Chuck's house. One of Uncle Chuck's cow's had just had a baby calf.

"Where did the calf come from?" asked one of the boys.

Ellen, who was always so intelligent, pointed and showed him the area on the cow where it was born.

"That's where babies come from, and on a girl's body too," she told him.

We all laughed as we got closer to look.

"Let's hide and show each other that place," one of the boys said.

"That's silly," Ellen said. "I'm sure not going to show you mine."

Then she turned and walked off toward the apple orchard, and some of the boys followed her. She acted as if we were people she didn't want to know anymore. One of the boys standing near me asked me if I would show all of them mine.

I remember thinking it would be fun! And I did want them to like me. Besides, not all the boys had followed Ellen off to the orchard. Some of them stayed there with me. And I had their attention for once!

We found some high bushes close to Uncle Chuck's house and hid so no one could see us.

"Let's take off our pants and play doctor," one of the boys said.

Playing doctor might be fun, I thought, because I finally had the attention of some of the boys, and silly ol' Ellen could climb up a tree with the others. *I'll show her*, I thought to myself. I was frightened that we might get caught, but it would be worth it. I liked having boys pay attention to me. I hoped we could do this every day. I would be with the boys, and Ellen would get a tummy ache from eating all those green apples.

Then suddenly we all heard a loud voice!

"What are you all doing in there? Come out this instant." It was Granny!

When she yelled at us, the boys jumped up, pulling their pants up as fast as possible, and ran off in all directions as fast as they could. Granny grabbed me and pulled me out of the bushes, and she swatted me on my behind the whole time she was pulling me toward her little house.

"Lori, what in the world were you doing behind those bushes with all those boys?" she said.

"We were going to play doctor," I answered her in between sobs. "We were going to find the area where babies came from."

Granny swatted me a good one then and told me to get inside the house and not come out for the rest of the day until she could talk to my mom.

Later that night, Granny pulled me close to her when we were tucked in bed and said to me, "Having boys touch you and feel your body is terrible. You won't go to Heaven if you do things like that; it's evil!"

Then she started reading the Bible to me again so I would understand that God wants me always to be good.

"Lori, if you ever allow things like that to happen, you will be punished. It isn't very nice," she said.

I thought to myself that it just didn't make any sense. How could anything that seemed to be that much fun be evil? It was fun, and best of all, those boys had been with me, not Ellen!

CHAPTER 6

Garden City, 1945

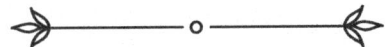

World War Two had ended, and my dad got to come home. Mom and Dad knew that we couldn't all live in Granny's tiny house, so they had to find a new place to live.

Mom had to give up her job as a nurse at the Okmulgee Hospital, and Dad would need to find a job. He did find one at an oil refinery in Garden City. Mom felt we were lucky because there was a nearby school that I could attend. Mom, Dad, my brother Terrell and I could now be a family. We could now be together and as happy as we were before, or so I thought.

Because there was such a housing shortage after the war, many families had to move into tents. Tent cities sprang up everywhere. Families had to move into them until they could find a better place. Our family was one of them. The tent we had to move into was on the school grounds where I would attend, close to Dad's job.

We were all so crowded living in that tent, but we were together. The only good thing I remember about that time was when I was attending school. I had a chair I could sit in, electricity, and I could wash my hands. I also had a bathroom to use.

After a very long time living in that tent, my mom told us that Dad had found a house for us to move to, and it was just down the street.

"Things will be better for us now," she said.

Boy, I sure did hope so! That tent was awful! Especially after living in a house with Granny and sleeping in her soft bed, I also had that red light that would put me to sleep each night, and I missed it.

It was August and the beginning of my seventh year when we moved into our new house. To me, it was the strangest house I had ever seen. It was just one big room that was on top of a garage. When the wind blew just a little, the whole house would sway. But it was better than that tent!

I began to notice a strange change in Dad. He was just not the same as before, and he was gone a lot at night.

Mom was also changing; she had started getting fat in her stomach, cried a lot, and was sick more often. Everything was different, yet we were all the same. It was hard for me to understand why everything seemed to change.

I could walk to my school, and because it was so close, Mom could watch me until I got inside. When I would come home after school, it was always fun to play with Terrell. We would play hide and seek, and I would chase him around the chicken coop just below the steps.

Dad had also made us a rope swing hanging from a large tree. We spent a lot of time in it, swinging back and forth, and then we would jump out of it when it got high.

The worst part I remember was that awful house! We were all just in one big room. Our beds, the kitchen, and everything were all crowded together. There was no room for any privacy for anyone.

I would cover my head at night and wish my granny could be there. I was hoping for things to change. Wishing I could listen to Granny read from the Bible instead of Mom and Dad fussing or his loud snoring.

I wished I could not hear my mom crying when Dad would come home so late at night. I wanted to turn the page in the storybook and make things different.

One day my mom said to me, "Lori, I'll be going to the hospital soon, and when I return, I'll bring two new babies home. Hopefully, a new sister and a new brother for you and Terrell. Granny will come again and stay with us to help me out for a while. I'll count on you to be a big help to her. You are growing up now, and I know you can help with Terrell. We will be one big family in this house, but it will not be easy. We will have to work hard to make it work."

I was so happy to hear that Granny would be coming to stay with us, and I was excited that I would soon have a new brother and sister. I hoped that things would then get better.

Mom came home from the hospital a few days later, and I remember looking at my new brother and sister for the first time. Dad was carrying them both up the stairs to our house, and they were both in one bassinet. I ran to meet him because I couldn't wait to see them. I remember how tiny they both looked, They were lying at each end of that little bed, and their small feet barely touched each other.

I hoped Mom would let me hold them. I was also hoping that this would now make Mom and Dad happier. I missed the big hugs from Dad and hated hearing Mom cry all the time.

My new brother and sister were so small. Mom didn't have a baby bed because there was no room for one, but she did have one massive dresser for everyone's clothes. She pulled out some clothes from a couple of the drawers and found that they made two perfect beds for her babies to lay in. Mom told me she and Dad had named them and that their names were Lee and Louise.

Granny came a few days later to help Mom, and I was happy, but things didn't improve; they seemed to worsen. With Granny added into that one big room, that didn't work.

When the twins cried for their bottles, everyone woke up, and when we needed to sit at the table to eat, baby items always covered it.

When Terrell and I felt silly, we had to be quiet or go outside. We were not one big happy family anymore. Everyone was either yelling or fussing or crying all the time.

I just wanted to find a field and get lost in it. I wanted to be where I could watch a butterfly or see a rabbit. But, there were no fields where we were living. Only factories with terrible smells and black smoke coming out of the tall stacks that would disappear into the clouds.

One day, Dad came to a big decision and said to Mom, "We have to have more room. I'll see if our landlord will let me fix up that old abandoned chicken coop downstairs so we can at least have more sleeping areas."

Dad worked hard for a long time on that chicken coop. I remember watching him put up new screens, paint everything with fresh white paint, and hose the entire area with soap and water. He was making that chicken coop look great!

Dad took me with him one day to buy us new beds. He purchased three army cots, one for me, one for Terrell, and one for Granny. We were happy to be moving into that chicken coop at night to sleep. There we knew we would not have to listen to Lee and Louise cry all the time. We would no longer have to listen to Dad snore or fuss at Mom and no longer have to smell all those dirty diapers.

Terrell and I were not afraid at night when we had to move outside in the open area because Granny was with us. She could no longer read the

Bible to us because there was no electricity, but she could read it to us in the afternoon when it was daylight. I didn't understand how that book could be so interesting to her.

Our life sleeping in that chicken coop lasted only a few months, but it seemed like a lifetime. Being with Mom and having fun with her was out of the question. It took every moment of her day to take care of the twins. Granny did what she could to help, and I did what I could to keep Terrell out of the way. It wasn't easy, but we all had a purpose in life and did our best.

Dad was working overtime a lot, and at night he drove a taxicab for extra money. Dad knew that we needed to find a bigger house to live in, and it would have to be one he could afford.

When Mom was walking the twins in their stroller one day, she spotted a couple moving out of a big house just down the corner from where we lived. Mom stopped to talk to them and found out they were planning to rent their home. After Mom had a long, friendly conversation with them, she managed to arrange for us to have a new place to move to.

Mom told them we lived in that one-room garage apartment, and her family needed more room. She explained that her husband worked at the factory and drove a cab at night. Mom told them she would love to live in their home, but it would have to be what they could afford. She got them to settle on an excellent price.

She also noticed an area large enough to maybe raise some chickens. The property had a huge garden area, which made her even happier.

Mom felt that her husband might enjoy raising chickens, and she and Granny would be able to plant some vegetables in the large garden area. Mom could hardly wait for Edward to get home that evening to tell him that she had found us a place to move, and it was just down the street.

Things changed for the better when we moved to that big house on the corner. Dad also changed jobs and made more money, and Mom seemed happier. The twins were now learning to walk and didn't cry all the time.

CHAPTER 7
Lori, Age 11, 1949

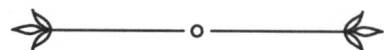

The twins were now three years old and more fun to play with, so I loved being around them. Terrell was now in school, and we could walk to school together. I made new friends and loved having the boys begin to notice me. My body was also beginning to change.

Granny, Terrell, and I had bedrooms to ourselves, with nice soft beds and not those stupid army cots. Granny had decided to live with us a little longer to help Mom with the twins. Granny always found time to read to Terrell and me from the Bible in the evenings before bed. I thought I was getting too big to have her read to me, but it made her happy, and it did make me get sleepy, just listening to the softness of her voice.

One day, my brother Terrell felt terrible, and Mom didn't want him to go to school. I knew I would miss having him walk with me because there was one place we had to walk that scared me. We had to walk through a railroad bridge with a dark tunnel under it. For some reason, it always felt spooky to me. That day, coming home from school, I knew I had to be brave and walk through it by myself.

I was supposed to be growing up, wasn't I? I knew it was silly to be frightened of a tunnel, but the closer I got to it, the more I had to force myself to keep walking. As I got closer, I stopped to see if I could see to the other side, but it was too dark. I listened to see if I could hear anything, but it was silent.

Why was I such a scaredy cat? Why did I feel there was someone in there? I felt like someone was waiting to grab me in the dark. I also knew that was the only way to get home. There was no other way. I clutched my books close to my chest, took a deep breath, and started walking forward as fast as possible, almost running. I could feel my heart beating.

When I reached the middle of the tunnel, where it was the darkest, I could see the light at the other end, but I could also hear someone breathing, someone other than myself.

Then a man's deep voice said, "What's your hurry, honey?" and someone grabbed me from behind. I felt his big hands go up inside the back of my blouse, and I screamed, dropped my books, struggled to get away from him, and ran like crazy toward home, afraid to look back.

I ran toward the chicken cages and called out to Dad, and then I ran into the garden to look for him. As I started running back toward the house to find him, I saw him standing near the front yard, looking at me.

"Daddy, a big man just grabbed me when I walked through the tunnel," I yelled at him.

Dad put his arms around my shoulders. I noticed that he was breathing hard as he said, "Did he hurt you?

"No, Daddy, but I dropped all my school books when I kicked him and ran away," I said.

"Honey, you go in the house with your mom, and I'll get your books and check out that bridge," he told me.

I knew my dad could handle anything because he was big and strong. *That man would be sorry he had ever touched me*, I thought to myself as I went inside to find Mom.

I found her busy with the twins and my brother Terrell. They were all sick with colds, and Mom did what she could to make them feel better. I told her what had happened and that dad had gone to the bridge to get my books.

"Lori, you have always hated that bridge. I tried to find your dad earlier to go and meet you there to walk you home, but I couldn't find him. From now on, I'll always make sure someone will meet you when you are by yourself, even if I have to go myself," Mom told me.

Boy, I sure hoped so. I didn't want to go through that again, ever!

Dad came walking up to us and handed me my school books. He told us if anyone was there, they were gone now, as he winked at Mom.

He looked at me and asked if I knew that bridge was magic. "Do you know I can even fly over it?" he said.

"Oh, Daddy, don't be silly. You can't fly," I replied.

"Oh yes, I can," he said. "Let's walk down there right now, and I'll show you."

Mom told us to be careful, so Dad and I walked hand in hand to that danged ol' tunnel. It no longer felt scary to me with Dad holding my hand.

"Now, Lori, you stand right here, close your eyes, and count to twenty real slow, and I'll fly to the other side. Now don't open your eyes until you are through counting," he said.

I closed my eyes tight and didn't dare open them until I knew I should. I would always do just as Dad told me. When I finished counting to twenty, I opened my eyes, and Dad was nowhere in sight.

Then I heard his voice from the other side.

"See, I told you this bridge was magic and I could fly. Now close your eyes and count to twenty again, and I'll fly back," he told me.

I closed my eyes again as he had told me, and before I could count to twenty again, he was standing there beside me with his arms around me, laughing as he said, "See, I told you I could fly."

I knew Dad could not fly, and that silly bridge was not magic. But whatever my dad ever said to me, I would accept. I would never question him because I loved him and trusted him completely.

As I lay in bed that night after listening to Granny read to Terrell and me from her Bible, I thought about what had happened to me and that voice I heard in the tunnel. I remembered that somehow, it sounded like my dad's voice.

CHAPTER 8

Tulsa: A Better Life

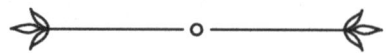

Afew years later we moved again, this time into a nice brick home in Tulsa. Dad bought a new car, and Mom was able to buy all new furniture and have it delivered to our new home.

Granny returned to live in her little house near Uncle Chuck, her son, and his wife, Aunt Sue. I missed Granny a lot. She was always there when I needed to talk to someone about what was going on in my life.

I also went to a new school I loved and made many new friends. I didn't miss that bridge tunnel, those chickens, or that garden. I liked the city life much better than the country life.

I was turning thirteen, and my mom planned a big birthday party. I had never owned as many new clothes before, and I loved all the pretty things she gave me.

Mom and Dad also gave me my first puppy on that special birthday. He was a cocker spaniel, and I named him Randy. Randy and I became inseparable almost immediately.

For some reason, Mom sent Dad to take me shopping to get my first brassiere for a birthday present. I'll never forget the day he took me. He told the clerk helping us that he needed a brassiere for me that would be about the size of two fried eggs.

I wanted to die on the spot, but Dad was having so much fun that he decided we needed to shop for some other things. He then started picking out lace slips, pretty dresses, and frilly underclothes for me. I went home with more than just my first brassiere that day.

I knew I was beginning to have a mature body and was taller than most girls my age. My hair became blonder, and I noticed I attracted the older boys. When any of them would ask me out, I wanted to go with them, but Mom would not hear of it.

"You are not as old as you look, Lori. They would not ask you out if they knew you were only thirteen. Just tell them they can call you back when you're sixteen," she said.

Mom could make me so mad at times! Her favorite thing was to fix my hair in pigtails or French braids and put ribbons in it. I would have it combed out before getting to school every day. I was unhappy when she would sit me down at night and rebraid it so tight that I thought my scalp would come off.

Terrell was growing up fast, and he was big for his age. He found a girlfriend who lived in the house behind us. Her name was Nancy, and I loved teasing him about her. He would get so mad at me!

Mom sent me off one day to look for him, and I knew where he would be. I knew I could find him at Nancy's house. It was fun having a little brother to tease. I found Nancy's parents working in their yard and asked them where Terrell was.

"Hi, Mrs. Irby, is Terrell here?" I asked.

"Yes, Lori, they are in Nancy's room playing games. Just go on in," she replied.

I walked inside Nancy's bedroom and opened the door, but I didn't see them. I did hear Nancy laughing from the direction of her closet. I slipped very quietly up to the door and opened it. I saw Terrell kissing Nancy!

"What are you up to?" I asked.

Poor Terrell, I scared him to death! He was up on his feet and out of that house before you could say BOO!

"Don't worry. I won't tell on the two of you," I told Nancy.

After that, I remember thinking of Terrell differently, and I knew I would never tease him again.

CHAPTER 9

Dad's New Job and Meeting Marc, 1950

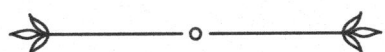

I knew that Dad had a new job, but I didn't understand it. I knew he was home most of the time, and our phone was constantly ringing. When it rang and he answered it, he would be gone for a while and then return.

On the weekends, he would leave in his car after dark and not return until early morning. I also noticed that once or twice a week, he would have some men over, and they would gather in the kitchen for some type of meeting.

As I lay awake in bed at night, I would try to listen to whatever they were talking about, or I would slip off to the bathroom to see if I could see what was going on. When I would ask Mom what Dad's new job was, she would tell me he was a salesman.

One night, late at one of his meetings, I saw that Dad was passing out whiskey bottles to all the men there. Bottles and bottles of whiskey! So that was what he was selling! I knew we seemed to have more money now, and Mom no longer had to work. I also knew I had a lot of nice new clothes now, so I didn't care what he was selling.

I was now in the seventh grade and enjoyed it very much. I had one very close friend, and his name was William. He was fun to be around and was always nice to me. He was not like all the other boys. He was friendly and kept his hands to himself. I had noticed other boys liked to brush against me or try to slip their arms around my neck. William was different, and I liked having him as my best friend.

I also discovered that I could talk to boys easier than to girls. I enjoyed their friendships more. Girls never seemed to say anything meaningful. With boys, you could speak to them about almost anything. William and I talked a lot, and we enjoyed each other. We always had lunch together, and he always carried my books for me. Mom liked him too, so she would let him come to the house in the evenings to visit.

We would play touch football on the field near my home, ride bikes, or sometimes sit and talk. William was in tumbling at school and loved trying to teach me some of his tumbling tricks.

He asked me to stay after school and watch his team learn how to tumble one day. I enjoyed watching them and noticed that most of the boys were cute in those white gym shorts.

One of them I noticed especially. This one had dark black hair and a lean body, and his skin was a dark olive. I also noticed that he was a much better tumbler than the other boys. I couldn't keep my eyes off him. I had to know his name and more about him.

After the tumbling class was over, I waited outside the gym for William so he could walk me home after school, like he always did.

I was surprised when William walked out of tumbling class with this cute unknown boy walking with him—the boy I wanted to know more about. I felt my mouth pop wide open.

As they got closer, I looked into those dark eyes, and my heart beat faster. Those eyes were a deep, dark brown, almost black, and that hair was coal black and curly. As he stood close, I couldn't get words out of my mouth— ME, who could always talk to any boy about anything. Nothing would come out!

For a brief moment, he glanced at me, then walked past me and ran down the stairs to go outside. By the time he got to the bottom of the stairs, I had regained my composure.

"William, who is that? I want to meet him!" I said.

"Marc, my friend Lori wants to meet you," he yelled down the stairs at him.

"William, I didn't want you to *tell* him that. Some friend you are," I said.

I froze as Marc ran back up the stairs taking them two at a time, then stopped just inches from me.

"Marc, this is Lori, a friend of mine," William said.

"Hi, Marc," was all I could manage.

He smiled at me sweetly and said, "Hi."

Then he turned and went back down the stairs and out the door.

William talked on and on while walking me home that day, but I could think of nothing else but Marc's dark eyes and that sweet smile, and I wondered if I would see him again tomorrow.

CHAPTER 10

Beginning of Fear, 1951

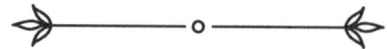

I felt very close to my mom and loved her very much, but I idolized my dad. Yet I was beginning to be afraid of him. Dad was always very strict with us, and all of the family knew never to cross him about anything.

At the same time, I liked being with him. Dad always told me jokes, and he made me feel grown-up. To him, I was unique, and I knew it. I knew I was his princess.

"My princess," he would say to me, "you are a stunning young woman."

I truly felt at times that he was a prince, my prince. And I knew I was his princess. Dad would be so tender to me at times. I loved him very much, but I was also aware of his temper and anger, so I feared him at the same time.

The first time I was truly aware of his violent temper was when he decided I needed to learn how to drive. If I didn't do just as he told me, he would yell at me and hit the dashboard with his fist.

"Lori, you will do it right, or we'll be doing this every night until you do!" he would say.

I became afraid of the anger I could hear in his voice. I would be in tears, hating to go back out the next night, but I would also look forward to it because I wanted to learn how to drive.

One evening I didn't drive across a bridge just the way he wanted me to, so he repeatedly made me back across it. It was a small bridge with wood slats high above a creek, and driving across it terrified me.

"You'll do this until you can do it with your eyes closed," he yelled at me.

So I would back up and do it over.

"Dad, please don't yell at me!" I told him with tears in my eyes. "I hate it when you yell at me!"

"Then pull over here by the side of the road," he told me.

As soon as I stopped the car, he reached over and pulled me close to him, shoving my face hard into his lap.

"Get all your cryings out of your system before we get home, or your mom won't let you learn to drive. You know she will fuss at me for making you cry, and I know you don't want to upset your mother. So, finish that silly crying right now, so we can go home," he said.

I was trying to control my sobbing, but Dad was holding my head tight against his lap, and I could feel a hardness I had never felt before. It felt bizarre.

"Okay, Dad, I don't want Mom fussing at you, and I don't want her to be upset, and I want to learn to drive," I managed to say.

I pulled away from him and quickly sat up to escape his lap.

"That's my princess," he said. "Now drive us carefully back home!"

I wanted to tell Mom what Dad did to me when we returned home. I wanted to be able to share with her my fear of him. But I was also afraid of telling her!

Sleep that night did not come easy.

The next day at school, I hunted for Marc. He was a quiet person and seemed to be very shy. It took me a long time to get acquainted with him, but I was determined. I looked for him in the hall and the cafeteria, but could not find him anywhere.

I found out from William that Marc played baseball during the lunch break, so I would then hunt for a table near a window to watch him play. It took a while for William to figure out what I was doing, and when he did, he decided he needed to tell me something. "Lori, You might as well give up on Marc. He has a girlfriend," he said.

"Who?" I asked him.

"Her name is Helen."

"Which class is she in?" I asked him.

"She is in Mrs. English's class, and Marc always meets her there," he replied.

That was all I needed to know!

That afternoon, I stood outside Mrs. English's classroom to watch for Helen, who I already envied. As the class let out, Marc walked by me toward Mrs. English's classroom and said hi.

He didn't even stop long enough to talk to me. He walked straight over to this petite, dark-haired girl who was very pretty. He walked right past me as I stood there. I hated her! She was everything I envied! Short, dark-headed, and tiny. Somehow I knew I had to win his friendship and take him away from her!

CHAPTER 11

Tulsa: Dad's Stock Car, 1951

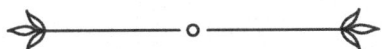

Since Dad started making a lot of money, he did some crazy things. He bought each one of us kids a horse. He kept them boarded and cared for at the horse stables at the fairgrounds in Tulsa. He also bought himself a stock car and started racing in the stock car races every Friday night. The more he got involved with the stock car races, the more he and Mom argued.

Mom was always busy at home, and our phones never stopped ringing. It was alright for Dad to be gone at night, but he made sure that Mom never had time to go out anywhere. That was just one of the reasons I knew they fought all the time.

One evening, I overheard Mom tell Dad that she wanted to take a trip to see Granny, Uncle Chuck, and Aunt Sue and spend a few days with them. But Dad told her, "No! You must stay here to answer the phones, and you know that!"

"I hate these phones! And I hate all these men coming and going all the time. Most of all, I hate you driving that stock car! I need some time away for a while!" Mom yelled back at him.

"Adella, remember that these phones and my business partners are why you have what you have today. Or would you like to move back to that one-room house and live as we once did?"

"I would rather you get a decent job, and it would be one that none of us would be ashamed of, but most of all, Edward, I wish you would just grow up and act like a father and a grown man."

That was a hard summer, and I remember it well. Every night when I tried to fall asleep, I would wish Mom and Dad would stop arguing all the time.

Mom had to stay close to the phones and was always busy with the twins. Terrell spent much of his time at Nancy's, and I stayed busy with my dog Randy or helping Mom with housework. Sometimes my friend William would come by in the evenings, and we would sit and visit or play baseball on the field next to our home.

When William was not there and Mom did not need me to help her with the twins or the house, Terrell and I would go with Dad to the stables to ride our horses. Sometimes Dad would ask me to ride with him so I could take a bottle of whiskey to one of his customers.

I knew the trunk of our car was always full of whiskey, and in between houses when he needed to make a delivery, he would pull up in an alley or a secluded spot and take a bottle out of the trunk and hide it in his shirt or coat pocket. Sometimes, he would have me wrap one in a sweater or a blouse that I was wearing, and I would have to knock on the door and slip it to whoever answered.

"Why do you always sneak it out of our trunk in the alleys? Why do you always hide it?" I asked Dad.

"You must do what I tell you, Lori, and not ask so many questions. Women need to do what men ask them to do." He also said, "I want you to learn how to please a man or a boyfriend in every way. I will teach you many things, but they must be just between you and me. You are growing up fast, and I'll be the only one you can trust and lean on to learn all these things. You and I can have a lot of fun, but you must remember that what you learn from me has to be kept a secret from everyone, including your mother."

That day Dad showed me how to drink whiskey straight out of the bottle without choking. I wouldn't say I liked it, but if that is what it took to make a boyfriend happy, I would learn to like it.

Dad also started driving me to school in his new stock car. He would pull over to the curb by the front steps, race the motor so it would make as much noise as possible, and laugh all the time he was doing it. He loved doing that so it would get all the kids to look at us.

"Dad, please don't do that," I would say to him. "It makes everyone notice!"

"That is what I want, Princess. I want them to notice you. I like showing you off," he said.

Then he would race the engine even more and peel off, leaving a cloud of exhaust fumes. I did get noticed, and I did like it! The boys always talked to me about my dad's stock car.

Marc was even there sometimes, and we talked to each other more. He started waiting for me each morning and soon met me in the school halls and after school.

Marc didn't talk much, but having him near me was terrific. Words did not seem necessary to him, so I accepted his silence. At least he was there with me. Sometimes we would sit side by side on the school steps and not even talk.

It was almost summertime by now, and I knew I had to try and keep in touch with Marc. I was afraid Helen would work on him and win him back. I asked him one day after school if he thought he and William might think about coming over to my house during summer.

"Dad will let you help him with the stock car, and we could go horseback riding on my horse if you want to," I told him.

Marc smiled at me and said, "You can count on it!"

That was all the encouragement I needed. I slipped notes to Marc in the school hall, trying to be everywhere I knew he would be. I found out when he would be tumbling and when he would be playing baseball. I found out everything I could about his locations.

Sometimes Marc would walk right by me, say "Hi," and keep walking, but I wouldn't let that stop me. I couldn't understand his indifference toward me when I seemed to have no trouble getting attention from other boys.

Marc was strange and very quiet, but that quietness seemed to draw me to him. I wanted to know what lay beneath those dark eyes and what he was thinking. I needed to understand why I couldn't get him to pay more attention to me.

William teased me a lot about Marc. "Maybe it's because you're taller than him, and he can't reach high enough to kiss you like this," he said. Then suddenly, he gave me a quick kiss on the cheek.

"Oh, William, you're crazy, and I promise you that you'll never get to do that stunt again unless you promise to bring Marc over to my house as much as possible during this summer," I said.

That last day of school ended with a promise from William that he would do his best and that I would see him and Marc soon.

CHAPTER 12

Growing Up Too Fast, 1952

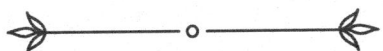

I turned fourteen that summer but felt much older in many ways. I did learn that bootlegging was against the law. That made me realize why most of my friends were not permitted to come to my house and why my mom encouraged me not to ask them to visit.

I also learned to take a puff off of cigarettes that Dad would have me light for him. I learned to ride a horse, drive a stock car around the race track, answer the phones at home, and take orders for Dad's customers.

That summer was also the first time I saw a man and a woman having sex together. I learned that the faith and trust I had always had for my dad was only a childhood illusion.

That summer was also scorching! No one seemed to be able to stay cool from all the heat. I spent most of the summer in shorts and a midriff top. I knew it showed off my body, which looked more like that of an eighteen-year-old and not a fourteen-year-old.

Dad would whistle at me and have me come inside the house to show me off to his delivery men. His bootlegging business was picking up, and he had hired some new men to make deliveries to his customers.

One was much younger than the rest, and he always stared at me. I will admit I noticed him also. He had beautiful blue eyes, and I noticed he kept winking them at me. I liked the feeling it gave me, but I also feared it. It would be times like that I could hear my granny's voice saying how evil I was being and reminding me that I was not going to heaven if I allowed terrible things to take hold of me. *It may be evil,* I thought, *but I like the feeling it always gives me inside.*

Mom had finally convinced Dad to let her make the trip to see Granny and Uncle Chuck in Okmulgee. She would take Terrell and the twins with her.

"I'll only be gone for two nights. Lori knows how to help you with the phones while I'm gone," she told Dad.

When Mom told me she would bring Granny back to stay with us, I was happy. I knew Mom needed to get away, so I was glad she had put her foot down with Dad.

I loved Mom very much, and I knew it would make her happy to get away for a while. She had fussed at Dad for so long that she needed a break. I was glad to know I could help by answering the phones and doing household chores while she was gone.

That first day that Mom was gone, William kept his promise. He and Marc came over to visit me. I asked Dad If I could hang around outside with them for a while.

"Sure, honey, tease them while they are here, but don't let things go too far. You still have a lot to learn that I need to teach you," he said.

"Oh, Dad, William and I are just good friends, and Marc would never touch me. He is more interested in baseball," I replied.

We had fun together that afternoon, just climbing trees and playing baseball.

When it was time for them to leave, Marc asked if he could call me the following week. He wanted to know if I might like to go to church with him on Sunday. I hadn't been to church since I lived with Granny, but I knew I would love to attend church with Marc. Besides, he would have to sit near me in church, and maybe I could at least get him to hold my hand.

"I would love to go to church with you, Marc," I told him.

After we said our goodbyes, I walked back toward the house to see if Dad wanted me to help with the phones for a while. I then noticed that my Girl Scout leader's car was in our driveway and was surprised that she had come to visit me. I liked her, and I trusted her. I had even confided in her several times about my fear of my dad. I had not told her what he had done to me, only that I felt uneasy when I was alone with him. I also told her that I didn't understand many of the things he would say to me. I was glad she was there and happy to see her.

I saw her, alright! She and Dad both! In Mom and Dad's bed, naked!

I stood there for a brief moment just watching them, not knowing if they had heard me or even knew I was in the house.

All I heard were the sounds that they were making. They were sounds I had heard from Mom and Dad before when it was nighttime. But this was not my mom and dad!

I watched as Dad climbed on top of her, and the sound from her mouth was strange. My feet would not move! I didn't believe my eyes. I was watching my dad and my Girl Scout leader doing evil things, and they were both people I had always thought I could trust.

I wasn't sure what I should do. Somehow I managed to get out of the house without them seeing me or knowing I had been there. All I could do was walk around outside in a daze.

I found my dog, Randy, picked him up, and carried him to the darkness of our garage. I held him close, talking to him, feeling like he understood me.

"Randy, you are the only one I can talk to and feel like I can trust. You're my best friend. I don't have to fear you, show off for you, or do anything to please you. I can always just be myself, and I know I can count on you," I whispered in his ear.

I cried and cried until I could cry no more. Randy kept licking my tears away, and I knew he understood.

I heard Dad's voice a few moments later, calling me as he walked toward the garage. "Lori! Lori!"

I stood up, wiped my eyes, and tried to make myself look better. I kissed Randy on top of his head and said, "Run along now, Randy. I'll be alright. You and I will keep what happened today a secret, and we will learn from it. Tomorrow will be a better day."

I walked past Dad as fast as possible, holding my head down so he could not tell that I had been crying.

"I'll answer the phones for you now," I told him.

I realized that very moment he was only a man, not the prince I had held onto in my heart for so long.

"Good, I need to take a nap!" he said as he walked back into the house.

I was glad my scout leader had left. I was so hurt by what she had done with my dad. There would be no more Girl Scout meetings with her, for sure!

Later that night, that cute young driver with those beautiful blue eyes came to our house to pick up some deliveries he needed to make. When I saw who it was, I left the room. At the young age of fourteen, I had already decided that most men were just jerks.

I bathed, went to bed, and fell asleep almost immediately. But during the darkness and the silence of the night, my bedroom was disturbed. I woke up knowing that someone was standing near my bed.

With my eyes still closed, I suddenly felt a pair of hands lift my nightgown, then slowly go up to the top of my leg. The hands started to touch the area that only I had ever felt. I then pretended to begin waking up, and the hands suddenly withdrew, and the body quickly turned to walk away.

As I fully opened my eyes, I tried to make out the back of the man walking out of the bedroom, but I could not. The room was just too dark.

I waited a few moments, then got out of bed and closed the bedroom door, locking it as I crawled back into bed. Sleep again did not come easy for me.

The next few days I spent listening to and enjoying my Granny! As Mom had promised, she had returned with her. I was so happy she was there. I realized I missed her, but being with her this time felt different from the past.

CHAPTER 13

Special Oak Tree

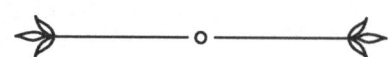

Marc did call me as he had promised, and he let me know that he and his parents would pick me up on Sunday for church. I wondered if I dared believe in him. He was not like all the other boys. The flutter I felt in my stomach as I went to the door when he came to get me told me differently. I just knew deep down that he was the one. I wanted him as my first real boyfriend.

As different as he was, I knew I had to make him interested in me. During the church service, I sat as close to him as possible. I wanted to feel the warmth of his leg next to mine. I tried to breathe as he breathed. Marc was not helping a bit, and when I put my hand where I was sure he would reach out and take it, he reached for the hymn book. He would move away when our legs touched for a brief moment. Nothing seemed to work for me, but I was not going to give up. I vowed, *Marc Lucus, you will like me if it is the last thing I do.*

I knew that afternoon would be a fun day because Granny fixed us a picnic lunch after church and gave us a blanket to sit on.

"Let's take it down by the Creek, Marc," I said.

He agreed with me, so we spread the blanket out near the creek and then laid out the sandwiches Granny had fixed. As soon as we got comfortable, Marc asked me, "Lori, what does your dad do for a living?"

His question took me by surprise, so I said, "He's a salesman."

I couldn't look him in the eyes, as that was the first time I felt ashamed of Dad's job.

"What does he sell?" Marc asked me.

"Oh, I don't know for sure, Marc. I think it has something to do with oil," I told him.

Marc was silent for what seemed an eternity. "Lori, I know what he sells, and so do my parents. They told me I could spend the day with you today, but I can't come over and see you anymore after today. My parents told me that what your dad does is against the law and that I can't come over again," he told me.

Looking at him and into those dark black eyes, I felt suddenly empty inside. Just how cruel could life get? It was not fair that something my dad did for a living could have anything to do with how Marc and I might feel about each other! I knew that what his parents had told him would change my plans to try and win him as a boyfriend during the summer. Why had so many different things happened to me so quickly?

Marc looked at me and then said, "Lori, I want you to know that we will meet and spend time together when school starts again. I just wanted you to know why I won't be able to come over with William and visit you this summer."

I felt like he was ready to lean over and kiss me, and when he was only a few inches away from my lips, I noticed Terrell peeking over the top of a fallen log, not fifty feet from where we were sitting. Marc saw him at the same time and pulled away from me as he called to Terrell, "Come and join us and have a sandwich!"

I was upset with Terrell but even madder at Marc for inviting him to join us. *Boys! They are all so stupid*, I thought.

When we finished our picnic and walked back toward the house, Marc said, "Let's stay outside for just a few more minutes. There is something I would like to do."

He led us toward a giant oak tree near my house and started climbing, giving me his hand to help me climb it with him.

"How long do you think this tree will be around?" he asked.

"Forever, I guess, Marc," I said.

He looked at me for a few minutes and said, "Then so will this!" He took out his pocket knife and started carving. First he cut a large heart, then he carved his initials and mine, carefully placing them in the heart's middle.

He looked at me when he finished, put his knife back in his pocket, and smiled. My heart melted, and the butterflies I continually noticed in my stomach when I was near him suddenly disappeared. In their place, a still, soft warmth swept over me. It was a warmth that I felt had to be the feeling of love.

CHAPTER 14

Dad's Bootlegging: Tulsa

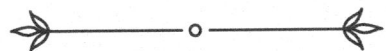

Our life never stayed the same. Once again, Dad decided that we needed to move. This time it was to a much bigger house with some land around it. Dad told Mom that he knew the twins required more room. Dad also said that Granny needed to come and stay with us again.

I later found out that Dad wanted us to move again because the police had caught up with him at our old address, so we needed to move to avoid them.

The house Dad found was still in the same school district, making me happy. I didn't have too many friends, and I sure didn't want to lose the ones I had. Most of all, I didn't want to move away from Marc. The only chance I knew I would have to keep him close would be while we were in school.

The new house sat on a hill with lots of land surrounding it. It was a large two-story home and looked very lovely. It didn't take me long to see what I liked about it.

Behind the house was a big open field. When Mom and Dad went inside to look, I walked toward the field area. The wildflowers were in full bloom, and the grass smelled sweet. The butterflies flew from flower to flower as the bees collected their pollen.

Whatever else happened to me, I knew I would now have a safe place to go. "Field," I found myself saying aloud, "you and I will have a lot we can talk about." Then I hurried back to the house to see what it was like inside.

"Lori, go look upstairs," Mom said and followed close behind me. As we reached the top of the stairs, she said, "This is where you and Granny can sleep."

It was one big bedroom with a private bathroom in one sunny and bright corner. Windows were at both ends of the room. I headed toward one end of the room and told Mom, "Mom, this is where I want my bed. Right HERE!"

Mom approached me, put her arms around my shoulders, and looked out the window with me. "This is a nice spot, Lori, but we must see how all the bedroom furniture fits first. We may have to place your bed over there," she said, pointing toward the middle of the room.

"No, mama, I want it right here!" I told her.

She looked at me quite puzzled as I had never spoken to her like that before. Without questioning me any further, she smiled and said, "Okay, honey, this is your first bedroom without your brothers and sister sleeping near you, so I guess you should be able to pick out the spot you want for your bed."

Mom didn't see what I saw when I looked out that window. She didn't see that big open field or the radio tower off in the distance with the light blinking off and on that would say to me, *Lori, go to sleep, Lori, go to sleep* every night.

My family stayed very busy for a while, moving us in and fixing our new home. Dad had decided we needed a few animals around, so he bought some rabbits, chickens, and a rooster for us to raise. He also started doing a lot of carpentry work around the house. I knew that Dad didn't have any job, so I thought he always kept busy because he was bored.

He made hidden drawers in the attic where Granny and I had our bedroom. He made fake bottoms on the deacon's benches we used around our breakfast table. Rafters that were in the barn turned into what looked like storage bins. He built false bottoms under the rabbit cages and in the chicken coops.

I had never noticed Dad working this hard before, and I wondered what he was doing. I knew that I was glad he was not selling whiskey anymore. It would be great now that I would not have to lie to my friends anymore about my dad's job.

Maybe Marc's parents would let him date me and come to my home and visit me if they knew my dad was no longer selling whiskey. But I also wondered why Mom was not saying anything about Dad getting a new job.

Summer was almost over, and our school would soon be starting. It had been a long time since I had talked to Marc, but not to William. When William called me last time, I told him where we had moved to and our new phone number.

William told me that he hadn't talked to Marc in a long time because his family was on vacation. "But I'll call him for you and give him your new number when they get back, and let him know you said hi," he told me.

"Oh, thank you, William. You are my real true friend," I said.

I knew I could work my charms on William and win him over almost every time!

CHAPTER 15

The Mean Rooster: Tulsa

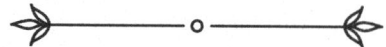

In our new neighborhood, I soon met a boy who lived nearby. His name was Charles, and he was rather cute. What I liked about him best was that he was taller than me. He started hanging around often when he saw me feeding our rabbits and chickens. I enjoyed feeding them and loved watching the rabbit's pink noses twitch back and forth when they smelled the rabbit food.

But I wasn't too fond of the new rooster that Dad had bought to keep the chickens happy. That rooster had a mind of his own and a mean streak. He would watch for me to enter the fenced-in area where we kept him along with the chickens and the rabbits.

The very minute I would turn my back to reach in and feed the rabbits in their cages, he would pounce on my back full force, flapping his wings and hanging on the best he could. I had to learn the hard way that I needed to carry a big stick with me when walking into the fenced area, so I could use it to try and scare him off.

When I was talking to Charles one day, I forgot to take my stick. That stupid rooster was waiting, and as soon as I turned my back to feed the rabbits, he pounced on my back and hung on for dear life. He seemed to know I didn't have that stick and could not fight him off.

"Run, Lori," I heard Charles yelling at me.

Charles then jumped the fence and came running toward me. He had my stick clutched tightly in his hands. He hit that rooster off my back with enough force to kill us both.

"RUN!" he said.

I ran and jumped the fence higher than I thought I could ever jump, but it was not high enough. I cut a big gash on my leg on the barbed wire that Dad had put across the top.

I saw that my leg was bleeding a lot. Then I looked up and saw that stupid rooster lying on the ground and Charles walking toward me with a big grin.

His expression changed when he saw that I had hurt myself. He took his handkerchief from his back pocket and placed it tightly on my cut leg.

"Here, hold this on it real tight while I get your mother," he told me.

Mom came out quickly and took me inside to clean and dress the cut. Charles followed us into the house and sat quietly watching.

"I may have killed that rooster!" he told Mom.

"Don't worry about it, Charles," Mom told him. "I'm just glad you were there to help Lori when she needed it."

Mom told us both that she was also afraid of that rooster but that he was a prize rooster, and Dad had paid a lot of money for him, so she needed to try and save him. I didn't care if that dumb rooster cost a hundred dollars—I hoped he was deader than a doornail!

Mom checked and made sure I was alright, then went out to check on that stupid prize rooster. I couldn't believe it when she returned with it wrapped up in a towel, placed it inside our bathtub, and started trying to revive it. I remember standing over that bathtub, looking down at that mess of feathers, and wondering what made me the maddest—Mom for trying to save it or that mess of feathers for not dying.

Charles asked me out later that week. He wanted to take me to the new drive-in theater in town. Of course Mom said no, but she did say that she would take us in her car. I didn't care what we did. Charles was just a good friend and had been very nice to me. Mom took us and allowed us to sit in the back seat together, which surprised me.

Charles did hold my hand during the movie. A few times, he would place his hand on my leg. It was dark inside the car, and I knew Mom couldn't see what he was doing, so I didn't try to stop him.

When the movie was over and we got back home, as Mom headed to go inside, she looked at me and said, "Don't be outside too long now, Lori."

Charles took my hand and led me to the side of the car, where he knew Mom couldn't see us from the house. He was taller than me, and it felt good just standing beside him. Then he kissed me. It felt funny, but I found myself kissing him back, and he pulled me closer—so close, I wasn't sure I would be able to get my next breath. The kiss Charles gave me was new and strange, but what I felt below his belt certainly was not. His hands reached up slowly under my blouse, touching my skin. Just then, I heard Mom's voice.

"Lori, you need to come in now!"

"I've got to go in now, Charles," I told him as I pulled away and fixed my blouse. "Will you come over again tomorrow?" I asked.

"Yes, I'll be back tomorrow," he said.

As I watched him walk away to go home, he didn't seem as tall to me as before.

When I reached our front porch steps, Mom said, "Don't go in yet, Lori. We need to have a long talk." She motioned for me to sit beside her on the porch swing.

"Okay, Mom, what do we need to talk about?" I asked her.

"First, I need to tell you about your dad's job. I'm sure you noticed that he had to stop selling whiskey for a while. But everything will be alright now. He is going back into the same business, but it will be different than before.

You will need to tell your friends not to call you often because our number will be a business phone when school starts. Your dad will be putting a lot of whiskey bottles around the house. They will be in all those places he has been building. We will need to keep all of it hidden as best we can. And if any policeman comes around and asks you any questions, tell them absolutely nothing. And if they ever ask to see your dad, or if he is home, come and find me first," she told me.

Mom had answered all my questions in just those few minutes of my conversation with her. Why had I not been smart enough to figure it all out? I was angry, but the look on Mom's face showed much more than anger. Her face showed pain, hurt, and sorrow.

"Alright, Mom," was all I could say.

I knew Mom didn't like Dad's job any more than I did and that she felt terrible about having to tell me these things. It did feel good to know that she trusted me enough to talk to me about it. As she hugged me, I sensed how hard it was for her to hold back her tears. That evening on our front porch, we formed a mother-daughter bond with just those few minutes of conversation. We both knew that whatever Dad told us we needed to do, we had to do it. Even if we felt it was wrong, we would do whatever he asked us to do.

"Did Charles kiss you goodnight?" she asked me.

"Yes, he did, Mama, and it felt nice!" I said to her.

"Lori, if you have any questions about boys, I hope you will feel free to always come to me and ask," she told me.

I knew I could talk to Mom about certain things because she had always been open with me on different subjects. She had explained menstruation to me long before my body changed and my monthly periods started. Most of my girlfriends at school learned those things from me because their mothers had not discussed it with them.

"You also need to know, Lori, that when a boy and girl get to be close, they will want to start holding hands and kissing. It's a natural part of what caring for someone of the opposite sex is all about. It can be beautiful if you control it and don't let things go too far," she said.

"How far is too far?" I asked her.

With hesitation, she said, "You have let things go too far when you feel a certain part of his body changing."

Mom must have seen the look on my face that said more than I wanted.

"Have you already felt this before?" Mom asked.

I wanted to tell Mom so many things at that moment. I wanted to say, *Yes, Mom, yes! I felt it when Dad shoved my face in his lap! Yes, I did feel it just now when Charles kissed me.* I needed to tell her I saw it with Dad and my Girl Scout leader when they were making love in her bed. I needed to tell her all the times I had felt it on Dad when he would hug me or take me with him on his trips. I needed to let her know that I was not a bad daughter. I was not evil like Granny told me I would be. But I couldn't tell her any of these things!

I was happy that Mom felt she could trust me and talk to me like a grown-up, but what would she think about me if she knew I had already experienced these things? How would she feel about me? I couldn't take that chance! She was unhappy enough with Dad. I couldn't make things worse by letting her know how evil I was. I loved her too much. I wouldn't be able to bear having her hate me for being evil like Granny said I would be.

"I did feel something tonight when Charles kissed me," was all I could answer.

"It's just a part of growing up and becoming a beautiful young lady. I'm hoping that you will learn not to let those things happen. You must be the one to stop them when you see the boy you are with is getting too excited. When you get a little older, you will learn to do other things, which should come later in your life. But it would help if you knew before then always to say no. Now, let's go inside and get some sleep. Tomorrow we will go shopping and get some new school clothes for you and Terrell," she said.

As I lay in bed that night watching my red light blink, thinking of what Mom and I had discussed, and drifting off to sleep, I seemed to feel a nice warmth. I felt like someone was holding me tight. It was not Charles or Dad who were in my thoughts. It was Marc who was holding me.

CHAPTER 16

Seeing Marc Again in School, 1952

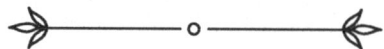

As Mom had told me, the phone started ringing off the wall, and the new delivery boys began coming over in the evening to meet with Dad. Our attic contained hidden whiskey bottles of all sizes, shapes, and forms. There was whiskey in the fake bottoms Dad had built all over the house. Whiskey was under the mattresses in our beds. Anywhere you could conceal a bottle, whiskey was there.

Granny and I tried not to notice what was going on. She and I stayed real busy in the kitchen. Granny started teaching me how to cook. I found it fun, and it kept us both active and out of the way. If a police officer would ask us if we knew where things were, we could honestly say we didn't know.

Mom and I went shopping for my school clothes the day after our long talk. I was so eager for school to begin again. Most of all, I was anxious to see Marc. I had not heard from him at all during the summer. I counted on what he said the last time we were together. He told me he knew we would see each other again when school started.

I wanted to hate his mom and dad for not letting him come over during the summer, but it was not their fault that my dad bootlegged. I knew they were only protecting Marc. Oh, how I hoped the kids at school would not find out what my dad did. Could I count on Marc not to say anything? Did William know?

I decided the best thing I could do was not make many friends. That way, I would not have to lie about Dad's job. It would be easier for me that way.

The night before school started, Mom found me in the kitchen with Granny and told me someone wanted me on the phone. "Make it very brief," she told me.

Puzzled, I picked up the phone and said, "Hello?"

"Hi Lori, this is Marc. Will you be at school in the morning?" he asked.

"Yes, Marc. Why?" I replied.

"I'll meet you in the front about 8:15 if that is alright," he said.

"Yes, Marc, that's alright," was all I could say. My heart was beating out of my chest!

"Okay, I'll see you then," he said.

As I hung up the phone, I couldn't help but notice the fluttering in my stomach again. The last time I felt this was when I was with Marc in the tree when he carved the heart and put our initials inside it. Why did this happen to me, just from his voice?

As I fell asleep that night, I could feel the warmth of his body next to mine, and I felt safe and warm.

When Dad decided he needed to drive me to school the following day, I begged him not to take me in his stock car. I told him that I would be in the eighth grade, and I was not a little kid anymore.

"Okay, Princess, I guess you aren't, are you?" he said.

Dad took me that morning in the family car, and as soon as we got in front of the school, he suddenly jumped out of the car, ran around to my door, opened it, bowed low, and shouted, "Allow me, your royal highness."

I climbed out of the car as gracefully as possible and held my head high, pushing past him. Just as I did, he reached out and pinched me on my butt and said, "Give the boys hell, honey!"

I couldn't help but smile. Dad could make me feel like a kid one moment and a grown woman the next. How could I fear him, not like him, yet love him all at the same time?

Marc was waiting for me as he said he would be, on the front steps. My heart pounded as I got closer to him. His skin had turned darker during the summer because of the sun, and he looked even better, if that were possible. He stood up when I neared him and smiled. My heart stopped as he handed me a small bouquet of white flowers. He had picked them for me from the bush in front of the school.

"Hi," he said. "How was your summer?"

"It was okay," I told him, "but it's much better now."

Everyone gathered around us as we slowly headed into school to find our classroom. Marc and I had no classes together because he was in the ninth grade. However, we did see each other during our lunch break and discovered that we would have our library hour at the same time. We tried to find a seat close to each other, but everyone had gotten there before us, so we could not sit close. Instead, we just made a few trips back and forth to the bookshelves so we could pass notes to each other.

I carefully opened one of the notes he had handed me, and it read, "Lori, I will try to meet you after school before my bus leaves if you will be at the front door."

As soon as the bell rang at the end of school, I ran to the front to meet him, but I was too late. His bus was already leaving.

"I'll see you in the morning," he yelled at me from the bus window.

That was the way things kept going day after day. We never seemed to spend time together, and we were never alone. We would pass each other in the hall and give each other notes during Study Hall, but none of his notes ever seemed to say anything I wanted them to say. He would never say he liked me in particular or wanted me as his steady girlfriend. His notes were always short and spoke of nothing personal.

I asked myself repeatedly, Why do I care for him so much? Other boys paid a lot more attention to me than he did. Why do I bother trying to get his attention? I should go out with some of the boys that ask me. But then I knew Mom would not let me go with them even if I wanted to. She still thinks I'm too young, and besides, who would I pick? Marc was the only one that I had in mind.

After a few weeks of school had passed, I didn't even see him at lunch. And when we were in Study Hall, he seemed to ignore me. I couldn't figure out what had happened between us. Then one day, I saw what had happened. I spotted him at the water fountain. He was close to dear, sweet, short, tiny, disgusting *Helen*!

I spent most of my time that evening after school in my field at home, crying my heart out. Then I talked myself into just ignoring him altogether. We were not anything special anyway! Who cares? He was only another disappointment. Life, it seemed, was quite full of them. Just when I felt like things would be alright, something would happen to knock the slats out from under me. It never failed!

Granny and Mom both wanted to know what was wrong when I got home from school that day.

"What's wrong, honey?" Mom asked.

I told them both that nothing was wrong. "I'm okay!"

How could I explain that I was hurting because someone I cared for didn't care for me? How would they understand that I felt insecure about

Marc barely speaking to me? I told myself I would have to forget about Marc. Something or someone different would come up, maybe tomorrow or the next day. It always did! But this time, it didn't wait until tomorrow!

CHAPTER 17

Understanding the Word "Trust," 1952

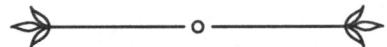

After I came in from the field that evening, I finished helping Granny with the supper dishes and decided to go upstairs to my bed and find a book to read. Maybe my thoughts about myself and Marc would get lost if I read a good book. As I flopped across my bed, trying to find one to get lost in, I heard Dad calling me from downstairs.

"Lori, come down. I want you to ride with me tonight. Grab your coat as it will be chilly by the time we get back," he hollered up to me.

I didn't want to go with him. I didn't want any part of what he did for a living, but I didn't want to stay upstairs reading a dumb ol' book either. Not in the mood I was in. So I thought, Why not? Just go on and go!

"Okay, Dad, just one minute," I yelled down at him.

I grabbed my coat and hugged Mom and Granny goodbye.

"Bye, honey. I hope you come back with a smile instead of that frown," Mom said as I left with Dad.

It soon got late and had turned dark. Dad had been driving for quite a while. We hadn't talked much to each other, but he told me that we would meet someone near the border of Oklahoma and Arkansas, and it would be about a three-hour trip.

"You don't have school tomorrow since today is Friday, so I thought you would enjoy the ride," Dad said.

I had watched silently out of the car window for a long time when he asked me, "What's the matter, honey? Trouble at school?"

"No, not at school, just with a certain boy," I told him.

"You know that you shouldn't be thinking about just one boy, Lori. It would be best if you were enjoying all of them. Which one has my princess so upset? Tell me," he said.

"Dad, I do enjoy my friendship with many different boys, but there is one that I just knew for sure would be special. But he acts like I don't even exist!" I said.

A few miles down the road, all I could hear was the sound of music from the car radio and the thump the tires made on the highway. Then Dad said, "Lori, I'll talk to your mom and tell her that you are ready and old enough to start dating. She doesn't realize that you are much more mature than most girls your age."

I knew that, but how did he know? "What makes you say that?" I asked him.

"Scoot over here closer to me and let's talk about that," he said.

He patted the seat next to him, and without me giving it any thought, I moved closer to him, to the spot he had motioned for me to sit.

"I know your body is developing into a woman because you have started your periods. And because of the hair you now have on your body," he told me.

"How do you know all that?" I asked him.

"I watched you when you were taking your bath last week through the keyhole in our bathroom door, and I know you are mature enough in your mind because you have kept a secret for a very long time. When you came near the bedroom door at home and caught me with your scout leader, I saw you standing there. That tells me that you are mature enough to keep a secret. That was a long time ago, and I have waited for you to say something to your mom or me, but you haven't, so I know you can keep things to yourself," he said.

There were a lot of questions I wanted to ask him at that moment, but I chose to be quiet and just let him continue to talk.

"I don't want you to be afraid of me, honey. I'll never do anything to hurt you. I love you very much. More than a father should love a daughter," he continued.

"I love you too, Dad," I said to him.

He put his arm around my shoulders then and pulled me closer. At that moment, I felt loved and safe, and I closed my eyes and drifted off for a few moments.

As I drifted to sleep, I remembered when I was with Bruce when we were sitting on the steps at school in the first grade. Bruce had put his arms around my shoulders to comfort me. Dad was now doing the same.

Dad's voice woke me as he said softly, "Lori, do you trust me?"

"I love you, Dad. Doesn't that mean that I trust you?" I answered back.

I was still in a daze and not fully awake from dosing off when I heard him say, "It should mean that, Lori, but it doesn't always. I need you to trust me always and that you'll keep whatever we say or do together tonight a secret, just as you have done with other things that have happened in the past."

I was unsure where all this was heading. "I will, Dad, if it's important to you," I answered.

"It is important to me, and it will be to you also. People will not understand, and I know it will greatly hurt your mother. It could also make me have to go to jail, so you must assure me that you'll never tell anyone!" he said.

I didn't understand what he was trying to tell me, but I did know that the last thing I would ever want to do would be to say anything that would hurt Mom or send him off to jail.

"What are you talking about, Dad?" I asked.

"Lori, have you had sex with anyone yet?" he asked me.

"No, Dad, I haven't! I have wondered about it and what it would be like, but Granny said it is evil for me to even think of those things, and Mom told me I should wait until I am married. Do the butterflies I get in my stomach when I am around Marc have anything to do with sex?" I asked him.

He laughed at me and said, "Honey, you can enjoy boys a long time before getting married and not worry about getting pregnant." He explained that I should not hurry to get married or have a baby. "Stay as pretty as you are, and enjoy yourself with the boys. Have lots of boyfriends, and wait a long time before you get real serious with them," he told me.

I thought I wouldn't have to worry too much about that. The one boy that I cared for wouldn't even hold my hand.

He took his arm from around my shoulders and grabbed my hand, holding it very tight and firm. He suddenly placed it on top of the area between his legs. I instantly tried to pull my hand away, but my strength was nothing compared to his. He held it down firmly where I knew it should not be.

"Lori, you said that you trusted me!" he said.

"But Dad, this isn't right!" I said in a frighted voice.

"That's why I told you that you must never tell anyone. Do you want me to teach you things about sex, or will you learn the hard way? Are you going to let yourself get pregnant and ruin your life? Or do you want to know how to make a man happy without taking that chance? Are you going to act like a child or a mature woman?" he said.

Dad's anger worsened, and I became frightened of him. I knew he had a temper and didn't want him to lose control of it. The road and the darkness in front of us seem to go on and on. I wanted us to hurry and get where we were going. I hated what was happening. There was nothing out there, but the darkness and the oncoming car lights suddenly seemed to take on a strange look, and ghostly figures seemed to bounce off the road, dancing along the white lines down the middle of the road.

Time had stopped for me. All I could see was Dad's anger building up. The more I tried to move my hand away, the tighter his grasp would be on my hand. I was afraid of what was happening. The soft-spoken voice I heard talking a few minutes ago had become mean, harsh, and demanding. It was like a voice I had heard before in arguments with Mom. It was like the voice I remembered when he was trying to teach me how to drive, and it was very much like a voice I had once heard in a tunnel.

"Learn to use your hands to care for the boy you are with, and you will not be hurt or become pregnant. Always give them pleasure like I am showing you, and make them understand that they cannot enter your body with theirs. You'll win any man you want if you do what I am trying to show you." he said.

My arm and hand were beginning to hurt because of his strength. "Please let me go! You are hurting me!" I told him.

He then released my hand and let me move away from him. "It's alright, honey. Please don't be afraid of me. I want you to learn what sex and life are all about," he said.

I learned that night, alright! I learned more than I ever wanted to! I would never tell anyone of this night. I would never want anyone to know how evil I had become. I was so ashamed. As soon as I could, I climbed into the back seat as far away from him as possible. Trust no longer had the same meaning to me as it had before.

We soon met the man at the border to pick up a load of whiskey. I stayed in the back seat and pretended to fall asleep on the way home. I wanted to sleep, but sleep would not come. Dad kept saying my name repeatedly, trying to see if I would wake up and talk to him.

When we reached home, I sat up to get out of the car as fast as possible, but Dad grabbed my arm before letting me leave. "Remember, Lori, not a word to anyone. I trust you, and you know I love you. You will always be my princess, so you must keep our secret," he said.

I knew from that moment on that I would never allow myself to be alone with him again, and the words "trust" and "princess" would never be the same.

After that evening, I managed to stay as far away as possible from Dad, and I made a point to plug the keyhole in the bathroom door whenever I bathed. I did my best to put out of my mind what had happened that night.

I would concentrate on Marc instead.

CHAPTER 18

Learning to Square Dance

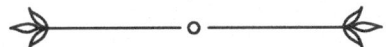

The weekend passed by slowly. All I concentrated on was Marc. If I saw him again in school Monday, would I try to talk to him or ignore him?

Monday came too soon, and school was in full swing. Marc leaned against his locker, looked straight at me, and did not speak. He was standing there with Helen.

Usually, he and I would study together, so I did things differently this time. I wanted to talk to him badly, but instead, I turned my back on him and continued speaking to William and the boys around us. *I will show him,* I thought to myself. *Who needs you?*

I was surprised during Study Hall when Marc passed me a note that read, "Hi, I wish we were back up in our tree. Love, Marc." That was all it said, nothing else! I looked around to find him, and he smiled at me when I did. That was all it took to melt my heart once again.

When classes had finished and the bell rang for school to be over for the day, I went to my locker and put my books away. I had been walking home from school a lot, and today I would be glad for that time alone.

My thoughts seem to sort themselves during those walks. I always enjoyed the fresh, crisp air and the sound of the dry leaves as they cracked when I stepped on them. Winter was coming soon, and I was looking forward to seeing my field at home covered in snow.

As I walked outside and down the stairs, I saw Marc waiting for me.

"Hi," he said.

"Hi, Marc. Aren't you going to miss your bus?" I asked.

"No, I'm walking you home tonight instead," he answered.

"That's nice of you, but won't Helen mind?" I hated myself the minute I let that come out of my mouth.

"Helen who?" he replied with a smirk!

"Your girlfriend, Helen!" I said, thinking to myself, *Boys are all so stupid!*

"She isn't my girlfriend. Have you forgotten about our big oak tree already?" he asked.

I was surprised at his answer, and as I was trying to decide what I should say, he ran a few feet in front of me, gathered up a handful of fallen leaves, then tossed them at me, running around like a little kid.

"Okay, if that is the way you want to play," I said.

I then gathered a handful of leaves and tossed them back at him. We chased each other back and forth, throwing them at the wind, laughing, having fun, and teasing each other.

On my way home, a grocery store was at the top of the hill. Marc wanted us to stop and have a soda. He bought us a small orange soda and a miniature pecan pie. I remember thinking that they tasted better than anything I had eaten in a long time. But I know it was because I was happy.

When we got to my home, Marc asked if he could call his mother. I listened to him as he spoke to her.

"Mom, I'm at Lori's house. I walked Lori home from school. Don't worry about me. I'll catch the city bus and be home in less than an hour," he told her.

I didn't know what his mom said back to him, but I knew how proud I felt that he had told his mom that he was with me and at my house. Regardless of what my dad did for a living, he was with me, and I was important to him.

After a few moments, we walked out onto the front porch and sat on the porch swing. I was bursting at the seams to talk about anything and everything, but I knew enough about Marc to know that he was not the talkative kind. I knew that he enjoyed his silence, so I just sat there to enjoy it with him.

Sitting there silently side by side, he finally spoke. "I need to go now, Lori, to catch my bus. I'll see you tomorrow at school," he told me.

"Bye, Marc. Thank you for walking me home. I hope you can do it more often," I said.

"I will," he said as he walked away, waving goodbye.

I watched him until he disappeared out of sight. *Somehow, one of these days, Marc Lucus, I'll get you to kiss me or hold my hand*, I promised myself.

Our days of school passed by too quickly. Marc did manage to walk me home several times a week, and just as it would seem that he might hold my hand or perhaps just put his arm around me, he would stop.

In the last two weeks of school, someone rolled a jukebox into the gym so we could all go there and dance during our lunch breaks. It took a lot of coaxing before I could get Marc to go in and dance with me. I thought at least he would have to put his arm around my waist. During our very first dance, I could feel the tension in him. The closer I got to him, the further away he seemed to hold me.

"I don't like this kind of dancing," he said. "I've heard that the school will be teaching square dancing this summer. Why don't we meet here during the summer and learn to square dance?" he asked me.

I would do anything he wanted to if it meant seeing him during the summer. I would even learn to *tumble*!

That summer, I stayed as far away from Dad as possible. I did my best to put out of my mind what had taken place the night he drove us to the Arkansas border to pick up whiskey. I concentrated more on just looking forward to being with Marc and learning how to square dance.

CHAPTER 19

My First Job, 1952

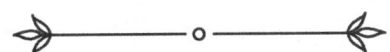

During the Summer of my fourteenth year, I told Mom I wanted to go to work. I knew she would be leaving the house off and on, just shopping or taking the twins to the park. That meant Dad would take care of the phones during the day while she was gone, and Mom would handle them in the evenings.

I knew that with Dad home alone, I needed to arrange to be gone during the day. I needed to find a summer job. Mom did not like the idea of me going to work, but I convinced her it would be okay.

I was lucky and found a job close to our home at a Coney Island restaurant. I was tall for my age and had a good figure, so I told the owner I was eighteen. I had no trouble at all getting the job. My hours were from 10:00 a.m. until 3:00 p.m., and it was within walking distance from my home. It was going to be just perfect. I would be away from our house when I needed to be.

Mr. Norman was my boss. After I had worked for him for a few weeks, he called me into his office. I feared he had found out that I was only fourteen and would fire me.

"Come in, Lori," he said as I entered his office.

I walked up to his desk, ready to be laid off. "You needed to see me, Mr. Norman?" I said.

"Yes," he said as he motioned for me to sit in the chair beside his desk. "How do you like your job?" he asked.

"I enjoy it a lot. It's just the right hours, and I enjoy meeting all the people that come in," I told him.

"I've been pleased with you, too," he answered. "I've noticed that your presence here has brought us a few new customers. Mostly younger men! Have you noticed that they are coming in more often?" he asked.

"No, Mr. Norman, not really!" I answered.

"Well, I have! My customers know a good-looking young lady when they see one," he said.

I felt my face flushing. Mr. Norman looked at me and smiled.

"I believe you are blushing. How would you like to start working for me late in the evenings?" he asked.

I was happy with the hours I was working. Square dancing lessons were scheduled for the evenings and would start soon, and I didn't want anything to keep me from being with Marc. I also didn't want to be home during the day.

"I would rather keep the hours I have now as I do other things in the evening," I told him.

"I bet you do!" he said.

He then got up from behind his desk, walked around, and took my hand, pulling me up from my chair and close to him.

"You and I could have some fun in the evening," he told me.

I was startled by that comment and pulled away from him quickly. "I'm sorry, Mr. Norman, but I'm too busy. All my evenings are tied up," I told him.

He stood there looking at me, hesitating for a few moments. "Okay, I thought I would ask you, Lori. If you change your mind or need anything, just let me know," he said.

I left his office as quickly as possible, knowing that I would have to make sure that I didn't ever see him alone.

Square dancing at school started the next week, and it turned out to be more fun than I thought it would be. Marc and I laughed at some of the silly mistakes we were making while trying to learn. His parents always brought him and picked him up. And my mom did the same for me.

When it looked like Dad might be taking me instead of Mom, I told him that I was meeting one of my girlfriends and that her parents would take me. Then I would walk to school. After dancing, I would walk back home. I felt much safer walking back home in the dark than riding with my dad in his car.

Weeks later, Marc finally did ask me out for an actual date.

We had just sat down to cool off after dancing right and left as you do in square dancing. I was getting dizzy and felt I was going to pass out.

"How would you like to go on a hayride with me Friday night?" Marc asked me.

I was unsure if the skip my heart took that moment was from square dancing or if it was from Marc finally asking me out. It had only taken him about a year and a half to ask me for an actual date.

"I'll need to check with Mom to see if she will let me," I told him. I knew she would let me go. Mom had come to like Marc very much.

"Okay, I'll call you tomorrow night to see if she says yes," he replied.

Mom did, of course, say yes. She could see how happy I was from him just asking me out. She said she would drive me to his house, but his parents would need to bring me home. It wouldn't be the same as an actual date, but close enough.

I was very nervous when Mom let me out in front of his home. I knew his parents disapproved of me because of what my dad did for a living, but Marc wanted me with him, so I knew I could face anyone or anything.

As soon as I knocked on the door, Marc answered. I was so glad to see him answer the door, not one of his parents.

"Hi. Come on in, Lori," he told me.

His dad sat on the couch reading the newspaper as he peered at me from over the top and smiled as I stepped inside.

"Hi, I'm glad to meet you finally. I've been hearing your name for a long time," his dad said to me.

I liked him almost immediately. He had a nice pleasant smile and seemed very friendly.

"Mom, Lori's here," Marc called out toward the other end of the house.

His mom stepped out of the kitchen area, wiping her hands on a cup towel, and after glancing at me for a few seconds, she looked at Marc and said, "Don't forget your sweater. It's getting colder in the evenings now."

Marc had to leave the room for a few moments to get his sweater, but it felt like he was gone for hours. During that time, Mr. Lucus chatted about the weather, and Mrs. Lucus stood there rubbing the skin off her hands by drying them repeatedly. I felt almost immediately that she and I would never get along.

While spending just those few minutes with Marc's parents, I noticed that he didn't look like them. His mother was redheaded with freckles, and Mr. Lucus was pale with brown hair. I had expected to meet a full-blooded Native American family because of Marc's looks.

"See you all later," Marc told them as he opened the door for us to leave.

"Behave yourselves," Mr. Lucus called out to us with a smile.

Mrs. Lucus was still there, wiping her hands, and said nothing.

"I like your dad," I told Marc.

"Come on," he said, taking my hand and running with me.

"Where is this hayride taking place anyway?" I asked.

"You'll see!" was his answer.

We were going on a hayride in the back of a neighbor's pickup truck. One of Marc's neighborhood friends, Jan, was having a birthday party, and the hayride was a part of it.

I noticed there were seven girls but only six boys. It seemed that Jan had not counted on Marc bringing someone with him. After Marc introduced me to her, I knew from her face that I was in no way a part of her birthday party plans.

"Jan, this is Lori. Lori, this is Jan," Marc said.

Marc introduced us quickly as we climbed up in the back of the pickup. Jan managed to place herself on the opposite side of Marc as we crawled in. She talked a hundred miles an hour the whole time we were on the way to the park.

After a short time, I felt I didn't need to worry about Jan taking Marc away from me because her mouth never shut up. Marc enjoyed his silence too much to put up with that.

Jan's dad drove us all to the city picnic grounds, and within just a few minutes, her dad had a fire started where we could all fix hot dogs and roast marshmallows.

Marc was very attentive to me. I thought he was the best-looking boy there. The glow from the fire began to feel very nice after the sun had set, and I found myself moving closer to the fire. I liked just watching its glare on the fire logs. Marc noticed I had moved in closer, and he asked me if I was cold.

"Just a little chilly," I told him.

I watched the flame from the fire in the reflection of his eyes. As we looked into each other's eyes, he placed his arm around my shoulders and hugged me close to him.

I was afraid to move! Afraid to breathe! Afraid to speak! I had waited so long for this moment. I wanted to hang on to it as long as possible. The warmth from his body went all over me within just a few seconds, as if he was on fire himself.

Then, for a brief moment, I felt fear. Twice before, I had felt this warmth, this inner happiness, and each time something had gone wrong. I didn't want this moment to end. I wanted everything to stop! I felt if I let go or moved away from him, something wrong would happen, and I began to shiver.

"Lori, you are shivering," he said.

He took his sweater off and placed it around my shoulders.

"Let's go get in the back of the truck out of the night air," he told me.

"Alright, Marc, I'm getting cold," I replied.

I couldn't tell him it was not the cold making me shiver but the feeling I had that something bad was going to happen.

We climbed up in the truck and snuggled as close as possible in the back corner. Marc leaned against the truck's back and placed my back against his chest, with me sitting between his legs. He pulled the sweater tight around me, leaving his arms wrapped around me.

I leaned back against him as he placed his cheek up against mine. We sat there, with him holding me, until my shivering finally stopped.

"That's better," he said softly in my ear. "I don't want my girl catching a cold."

"Am I your girl, Marc?" I asked.

"Of course, you are, Lori. I thought you knew that" he said. "I want you to be my steady girlfriend."

He then removed his Boy Scout ring from his finger and placed it on mine.

"Will you be my steady girl?" he asked me.

I was in total shock! I had not expected that to happen at all!

"Yes, Marc, I'll always be your steady girl!" I answered.

Just as I felt him hug me tighter and turn me toward his face, Jan climbed up into the back of the truck with us. "There you two are. I knew I would find you here. I just turned my back for a few minutes, and you both were gone. I told myself, I know where they are, they are probably in the back of the truck, in the dark, where nobody can see them, and sure enough, here you both are. Marc, aren't you chilly without your sweater? She doesn't need it; you should be wearing it yourself!" she said.

Oh my gosh, I wonder if she ever quits talking? I thought.

"I'm just fine," Marc told her, still holding me tight against him.

"Well, I'm ready to return home anyway, so I'll get everyone. Don't you two go anywhere else now; I'll be back in an instant," Jan told us.

Jan then jumped out of the truck, yelling at everyone to get ready to return home so we could have cake and ice cream. Marc and I both giggled so hard that we both started shaking. I leaned back on him as close as possible on the ride back to Jan's house.

I closed my eyes and did my best to shut out Jan's voice as she talked on and on. As she continued talking, I stared down at that beautiful Boy Scout ring that Marc had just placed on my finger.

To me, there was no one else around but Marc and me. I could feel his chest as he took each breath. His lips were within inches of mine, and I ached for him to kiss me. If this could go on and on, I told myself, I wished we could drive on forever!

"Marc," I said softly to him without opening my eyes.

"Yes," he answered.

"I'll be your girl forever and ever, no matter what or where life takes us, and no matter what may ever happen to separate us," I told him.

"Now, just what do you think can happen?" he asked me.

"I'm not sure, but just remember what I said," I replied.

Marc's dad drove me home from the hayride when we returned to his house. When Marc walked me to my door, he did not kiss me goodnight. But I was happy that he had told me he wanted me as his steady girlfriend, and I had that wonderful ring on my finger. To me, that was all I needed. Kisses I knew would come some other day.

I felt very close to him that evening on the hayride, and I somehow knew I would always be his girl no matter what might happen. Tomorrow was going to be beautiful, and everything would be alright. Before I went to sleep that night, I wrote in my diary.

TONIGHT

Tonight I felt the warmth of his arms,

And it was such bliss.

I felt as though we were one

Yet he did not seal it with a kiss.

I know that I am his, and he is mine—so

Why do I feel it will only be for a short time?

CHAPTER 20

Jail Time for Dad

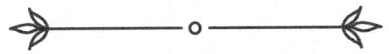

The last week of July had become sweltering. I had just gotten home from work and changed into shorts and a blouse. I decided to walk out into the field, perch myself under a shade tree, and read. I felt more relaxed in the shade as long as a breeze was stirring, and today one was.

The leaves on the trees seem to be dancing gently. It had been almost two weeks since the hayride, and Marc and I had not seen each other. He now had a part-time job mowing yards and working at a firecracker stand. I was looking forward to school starting again, when I knew we could see each other daily.

Just as I had put my thoughts into the book I was reading, I heard something going on toward our house. I saw Mom and Dad standing in the driveway with several strange men. I could tell they were not delivery men; they all wore business suits. Something was up; there was too much activity going on. My curiosity got the best of me, and I had to see what was happening.

I closed my book and started toward the house just in time to see several more men coming out of our house carrying bottles of whiskey. Then a couple of police cars pulled up in the driveway, and police officers headed toward Dad. They had him handcuffed and put him in the patrol car; when I reached our house, Mom was yelling, "No, you can't take him in, *no!*"

Two police officers held Mom's arms while the other officers gathered all the whiskey from the garage, the house, the rabbit cages, and the garden—all the places where Dad thought he had it hidden.

All I could think to do was to go to Mom. She somehow realized that I was standing beside her and regained her composure.

"Please go inside and stay with Terrell and your brother and sister. Everything will be okay," Mom told me.

I looked at Dad, who was handcuffed and now in the back of the police car. His eyes met mine for a brief moment, just enough for me to see in his eyes that things would not be okay!

I went inside as Mom had asked me to do and tried to see what I could from the kitchen window. I saw the police car drive off with Dad in the back seat.

Mom came into the house with two officers and talked for a while. I could tell she had calmed down a lot. After they left, she told me, "Dad will come back home tomorrow. A judge will release him on bond, and he can go home. We will have to wait to see what happens next. Dad will have to get a new job that will not make us feel ashamed—being caught and put in jail may turn out to be the best thing to have happened. There is always a reason for everything that happens in our lives. I have been trying to get him to change jobs for a long time. I am glad it happened this way! I hope it scares him enough to decide that he needs to find a decent job as other men have."

Mom sounded sure, relieved, and confident that this would work out for the best.

Dad did return the next day, just long enough to let us all know that he had been found guilty and, along with paying a hefty fine, would have to serve a one-year term in the county jail. The judge released him on bond just long enough for him to come home so he could arrange to move all of us to another town.

One of the first things Dad did was tell Mom she would need to get Granny, who lived in Okmulgee. Granny would need to live with us for a least a year to take care of the twins and Terrell. Dad also told Mom that she would have to work to provide for the family.

"Lori can stay here and help me get things packed. I'll rent a truck to move all our things. Lori and I'll have everything ready to go when you get back," he told her.

"Mom, please let me go with you to get Granny. You will have your hands full with the twins, and I can help you," I said.

"Lori, you can be of more help by staying here and helping Dad. You can pack up all the kitchen. I need that help more than I need with the twins, and they will sleep most of the way anyway," she told me.

Mom could see the confusion in my eyes.

"I know you are upset, Lori, but we will make things work. You are the oldest, and I'll have to ask you to do a lot to help me sometimes. Please stay and help your dad, and do what you can," she said.

I could sense her pain and see the hurt in her eyes.

"Alright, Mom, I'll help the best I can," I told her.

I watched as she drove out of the driveway, knowing she didn't understand my fear of being alone with Dad, the man she loved dearly. I wanted to run after her and keep on running.

I needed to talk to Marc. I needed to tell him that we were moving again and that I would send him our new address as soon as possible. Dad had already disconnected our phones, so I had to run next door to our neighbors' house to use theirs.

Mrs. Lucus answered the phone, so I asked if I could speak to Marc. She told me that he was not there and was mowing yards.

"Mrs. Lucus, I must talk to him. Please ask him to come to my house as soon as possible, and tell him I called and it is important," I told her.

I then rushed back home to do what I had promised Mom I would do. I only hoped that Dad would stay busy and stay away from me. I was afraid to be alone with him. It had been a long time since he had done anything to me, and I sure didn't want to take any chances. I kept myself busy in the kitchen while he was off in the other part of the house.

It had been several hours, and I still had not heard from Marc. I was wondering if maybe Mrs. Lucus had not given him my message. So I ran next door and called again.

"Lori, he isn't here. He is still mowing Mr. Hine's yard. I'll give him your message when he gets home," she told me.

"Please let him know that my family has to move again and that I'll let him know where we are as soon as I can, and for him to please remember our last conversation," I said to her.

"I'll give him your message, Lori," she said and hung up the phone.

When I got home, I stayed busy, and I was glad Dad had a lot to do. He had not said much to me, so I was happy. But I did notice that Dad was drinking a lot. I also noticed that it was from the bottle he had found hidden in the kitchen cabinet.

"Dad, you need to leave that bottle alone. Mom is counting on us to have things done before she returns, and you won't be in any shape to help me if you keep drinking," I told him.

"Now, Princess, I'll not have any of this for over a year, so I want to enjoy it. Don't worry your pretty little head about me," he said.

Just then, he started moving toward me, holding the bottle in one hand and reaching out for me with the other. I quickly shoved a box in front of him so I could get away.

"Princess, I need you to understand that I am sorry it all happened this way. I was sure we would be okay, but this new chief of police is clamping down on all bootlegging. But I have a lot of customers in the city office, so maybe it will not be as tough on me as it could be. This new chief doesn't know me, so I'm afraid it will be harder on Mom and you kids than on me," he said.

I could see he was under a lot of stress, which was not like him. Dad always was the happy-go-lucky type. He had jokes to tell you and could always make you laugh. I almost reached out to him briefly, but I knew I couldn't take that chance.

He stopped coming toward me, took another drink, and spoke to me again. "Honey, I want you to understand why I'm moving all of you so far away from your friends. What I have done may look like I'm being mean to all of you, but it will be in the Tulsa paper tomorrow about my arrest, and everyone you know and everyone Mom knows will be aware of what I have been doing for a living.

"The judge handling my case, Judge Olson, is my friend," Dad continued. "He told me that he would arrange for all of my family to move into a house that he owns and has up for sale out in the country in another town. He suggested that my family could live there while I am in jail. Judge Olson also told me that a school bus would pick you and Terrell up in front of the house. He will only charge Mom very nominal rent, and all of you can fix it up while you live there.

"None of the people you will meet will need to know anything about me or where I am, and it will be easier for you and your mom. You won't have to answer questions or face all the talk that you would if you stayed where we live now. And besides that, it can be fun living in the country," he explained.

"Oh, Dad, I hate it already! Why can't you have a job like other fathers do? Why did you get into all this mess?" I asked.

I ran upstairs to shut myself up in my room. Away from Dad, away from everything.

Dad had already packed everything in the upstairs room where I slept, and the only thing left was the old cot mother had put out for me to sleep on. I had once slept on the same cot when we lived in that chicken coop.

I hated everything that was going on in my life! I wanted to run to my field and hide. I needed Marc, so he could make me feel better.

As I tried to fall asleep, I remembered when Marc's arms were around me and the feeling I had then that something was going to happen.

I cried until I could cry no more. My eyes were swelling, and my nose would not stop running. I was ready to die! I wanted to! Then I felt a nice warm, wet tongue licking my face. My dog Randy had found me, and I felt a little comfort.

CHAPTER 21

Pryor: New Home

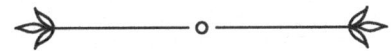

Within just one week, our lives had changed entirely. I stood there looking at what would be our new home, and I felt my family was being punished because of the evil things I had allowed to happen to me. Was all of this my fault?

The house stood alone in the middle of nowhere, away from any town or neighbors. It was a small frame house with paint showing up only in blotches. The window screens were either falling off or hanging by a hinge. All it would take would be a slight wind to blow them off. What looked like it might at one time have been a screened-in porch ran along one side of the house.

Behind the house stood the remains of an old shed that had probably been a chicken coop at one time. It seemed to be leaning to one side. A large outhouse sat alone down a path, and its door was about to fall off. Just outside the back door of the house stood a water well. I learned that would be where we would get our water.

I didn't want to go inside! I felt I would be alright if I stayed outside in the open air. I honestly thought I would not breathe if I went inside that house. I decided instead to follow the path toward the outhouse. I was angry for being sent here. I fought the weeds and bushes tearing at my legs, and I could no longer control my tears.

Why did this happen? If I had not been so evil, my mother would not have been so unhappy, and my brothers, sister, and Granny would not have to live in this terrible place.

Granny had been right when she read those verses to me from the Bible. She was right when she told me, "If you do wrong and do evil things, you will always get punished."

But why, I asked myself, should my whole family be punished with me? I started running as fast as I could. Away from that house, away from my mom and family, away from life.

The blackberry bushes tore at my legs, and I tripped and fell. I lay there sobbing, trying to wipe the blood away. I was glad that the judge had sent Dad to jail. I hoped he would never get out. I just wanted a place to run to, a place to hide, so I could make everything go away.

I didn't have Marc anymore. There was no William or Charles who lived nearby. There seemed to be nothing in this godforsaken place except blackberry bushes and that shack that would be our new home.

I knew I needed to go back to help Mom. I knew I had to do what I could to help her with this mess. I felt it was my fault she was here. I had to help her!

When I got enough control of myself to head back, I lifted myself from where I had fallen and spotted a small wild rabbit in the bushes a few feet ahead of me. It just stood there looking at me. I had disturbed the quietness, and I had frightened it.

After a few seconds, it started hopping away. After going just a few feet, it stopped and looked back at me as if to say, *Come on with me!*

"Oh, little rabbit," I said out loud. "Let's see where you run off to hide. Let me know where you go to feel safe."

As I followed behind my newfound friend, we reached the top of a small hill. That little rabbit hesitated for a last-minute glance at me and then continued. I couldn't believe what he had brought me to see.

When I reached the top of the hill, I could look ahead of me, and for what had to be acres and acres, there was nothing but beautiful open fields, thick with what looked like wheat. It was bending slightly with the gentle breeze and smelled so sweet. I opened my mouth to see if I could taste it in the air.

At the foot of the hill stood the most magnificent red barn I had ever seen. It looked out of place. There were no homes close by other than our house. It just stood alone, firm and very proud. It looked freshly painted as if it were new, yet you could tell it had been there a long time.

The little rabbit stood still as if it were waiting for me. It then disappeared into the barn doors that led to the inside. I could smell the beautiful fragrance of hay.

As I slowly entered, my eyes tried to take everything in at once. A ladder led up to a loft at the top of the barn filled with hay. Somewhere in the corner, my friend the rabbit had disappeared.

"Oh, thank you, Mr. Rabbit, you have led me to a great spot, and I love you!" I shouted.

I had just started up the ladder to the loft when I heard Mom's voice calling me. I knew I had to go back and help her, back to that awful house. But now, I knew it would be easier. I had found a new friend and a magnificent, beautiful-smelling red barn. It was a barn that stood alone and proud. Someday, somehow, I would do the same. Maybe tomorrow!

CHAPTER 22

Life Gets Better

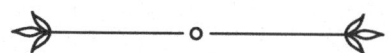

There was a lot of adjusting that all of us needed to do. Mom had to go to work while Granny did what she could to keep the twins and Terrell and the house in order. We had electricity but no running water. There was no phone or bathroom. We all had to take our baths in a small washtub on the porch. We washed our clothes by hand and hung them on the fence to dry. We all had to do things much differently than before.

Judge Olson, the judge that had sent Dad to jail, was the one who owned the house. He did send help to repair the broken screens and replace the broken steps on the front porch as he had told Dad he would do.

Judge Olson also had painters come and paint the house inside and out. All of us got busy helping to clean and paint. We worked until we thought we would drop. But we were slowly turning this house into a decent place to live.

When Mom was home and not working, she fixed curtains for the windows and did the best she could to make our house look better.

"We have to keep trying, Lori," she said to me one evening.

I think she could sense that I was ready to give up!

I felt so proud of Mom! She had found a job as a nurse in Pryor, where Terrell and I would be going to school. She would make enough money to keep us all fed and pay the small rent.

I loved watching her get ready for work. Her nurse's uniform was white. So were her hose and her shoes. She always looked so fresh and clean. I loved just sitting on her bed and watching her get dressed.

It was a long drive back and forth to work for Mom since we lived out in the county, and it would seem like forever before she would get home in the evenings, so I spent as much time with her as I could.

When Mom returned from work, the twins were already in bed and asleep, but she would always go in and kiss them and tuck the covers in around them. She would then check on Terrell to see if he was sleeping.

What little time she had before she went to bed and fell asleep was mine. I could tell her what the twins had done that day. I would also tell her how Granny and I had spent our day, and then she would say to me the different things she had been doing during her day. But I could also hear in her voice that she was missing Dad and that she was lonesome.

It was so hard for me to understand why. Dad was the reason that we had to live like this. Dad was the main reason she had to go to work and be away from her children. I wanted to tell her many times, *Mom, you should hate him! You would not want him back then, and you would not miss him.*

I knew Mom would not understand. She did not know that I feared him. Yet sometimes, I did miss the strength of his arms hugging me close and always calling me his princess. I wanted so bad to be someone's princess. I wanted someone to hold me close. But not him!

Before bedtime, when the sky was clear, I would watch the stars at night as they twinkled in the darkness. I wondered if Marc might be looking at the same ones as I was.

Sometimes in the evenings, when the moon was full, I would sit in the barn's doorway and watch the fireflies as they flickered in and out of the wheat fields. I wondered what life would be tomorrow, the next month, the following year.

We had lived there for almost two months, and summer was almost over. I still had not met anyone close to my age. Our school would start soon, and I would be in the ninth grade. I had no idea what the school looked like as Mom had not found time to drive us into town. I wondered if any of my classmates would know what my dad did and that he was serving time in jail. How could I face them? What would I say to them?

I waited up late one night for Mom to get home from work. I had to talk to her. She had to know my fears and my doubts about going to school. Maybe she would let me stay home, help Granny with the twins, and not even go to school. I had to talk to her about the possibility. That evening I met her at the car and walked inside with her.

"Mom, I need to talk to you about my school," I told her.

She looked at me, and I could see how tired she was.

"Lori, it has been a long day, and I go back on duty early in the morning. Let's not talk about it tonight. A friend told me about a place close to us that I'm taking all of you to this weekend, and we can talk then. It is supposed to be a lovely place to play and swim. I found out that a lot of kids your age will be there. We can pack a lunch and spend the entire day, and then you and I will have time to have a long talk. But not tonight, honey. I'm so tired, and I need some sleep." she said.

Poor Mom, she looked tired. I kissed her good night, helped her crawl into bed, pulled the covers over her head, and then left quietly.

As I slowly drifted to sleep after tucking Mom in, I imagined clear, ice-cold water falling in cascades off a hill into a deep stream that flowed slowly and gently over my feet, making no sound.

New hope started for me that day, the day of our picnic. We were all loaded up in Mom's car. Granny, Terrell, the twins, my dog Randy, and I were ready to go.

It was going to be a fun day, and just getting out to see what was near where we lived was going to be an adventure. The road was a dirt road full of ruts worn deep from rain. It seemed no wider than a path as it wandered around the countryside as if it would take us nowhere. Far ahead of us, we could see small hills and tall green trees getting thicker and thicker.

As Mom drove on slowly, we all wondered what was hiding behind those trees. When we turned the bend in the road, it was almost like finding a secret hiding place. There were people and cars everywhere. People splashed and ran around in different directions in the beautifully clean, clear water, just like the dream I'd had a few nights ago.

Mom had told us to put our bathing suits on under our clothes before we left the house, and we were so glad we did. We all hurried to jump out of the car and into the water, and Granny joined us. She was holding up her dress and waded out as far as possible. The smile on her face was beautiful as she stood there in the water, holding her hands up to the sky!

"He leads me beside quiet waters; he restores my soul!" she said loudly.

I was sure that was a quote I had heard her read to me from her Bible.

It didn't take long before I met some of my future classmates. I found out this was the hangout spot for all of them. Later in the day, one of the boys asked me where we lived and what my mom and dad did besides farm. I told him we did not live on a farm. We had just moved to the country because we were tired of living in the city.

I also told him that my mom was a nurse and my dad was a salesman for a Texas company. I went on to say that my dad was not at home very often. He is only home once or twice a year and only for a week. It was easier to tell him that than the truth. I hoped I would not have to worry about any more questions.

I also met a couple of twin boys, and it was easy to converse with them. I found out they would be riding the same school bus I would be on. They told me they would help me find my way around school because they would also be in the ninth grade. I liked them both. They were fun and friendly. One of them told me they only lived about three miles from my house and would ride over on their horses one day and take me riding.

Things suddenly seemed much better. I didn't need to have that talk with Mom. I was now feeling eager for school to start and to have fun again.

I spent a lot of time waiting for the twins, Jeff and Jim, to come riding down the road in the evenings during those last few weeks of summer. They spent a lot of time teaching me about living in the country and how to ride a horse.

During the short time left before school started, we spent time chasing through the wheat fields on horses and exploring the barn. We picked blackberries and went swimming on the weekends at Spring Creek. We talked about everything. I began looking forward to school and was eager to get up each day and start the morning.

Life was looking better now that I had some new friends. Maybe school would not be so bad after all.

CHAPTER 23

Football Queen Contest, Pryor High School

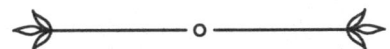

When school started, I did what I could to make as many friends as possible. I joined all the activities that were available to me. I wanted to be a part of everything possible.

After several weeks, though, I found myself holding back again, and somehow I felt like someone was watching me. As if maybe they had all found out about Dad. I wondered if they could see into my mind and know that bad things had happened to me.

I quit trying to make friends, became more careful, and stayed more to myself. I didn't want them to start asking me questions that I didn't want to answer. Somehow, no matter what I did to change things, I still sensed that people talked about me behind my back.

Jeff and Jim had never questioned me about things since our first meeting. So I decided that I would be content with their friendship. I wanted to be popular with the rest, but not if they would not accept me for who I was. Giving in to them would be weak, so I held my head high, smiled at everyone, and worked hard on my studies.

So what? I told myself. *I will be someone one of these days. I will not be bad anymore, and it will take time for me to be someone important, but I WILL!*

In the third week of school, on a Monday morning, it was announced on the loudspeaker system that we were going to have a general assembly in the gym. All students were to attend the meeting. The freshman, sophomore, junior, and senior classes would announce their nominations for Football Queen.

I had just put my books away in my locker and was headed for the gym when Jeff and Jim walked up beside me, each taking one of my arms.

"Today, you will be sitting with us," Jeff told me.

"And from now on, if I have anything to do with it!" Jim said.

I ran ahead of them, laughing, and said, "You will have to catch me first."

I ran to the gym, climbed up to the very top steps of the bleachers, and sat down, trying to catch my breath, when both caught up with me and sat down, one on each side.

A warm, safe feeling spread through me as I sat between them. *How can something that feels this good be evil?* I thought to myself. I loved the warmth of a boy's body next to mine.

The principal started talking to us, but my thoughts were not about what he said. I began thinking of Dad. It had been almost five months now since he went to jail. Mom had been talking to him lately about possibly getting out sooner than expected.

I wondered if we would move back to Tulsa, and if Marc would still be there. Would he even remember me? If so, would he ever talk to me again? Would he ever want to kiss me or hold me to make me feel warm inside? Could I face Dad? Would I ever feel safe around him? My mind was not on what was going on around me, and then I felt Jeff shaking me,

"Lori, I believe that is you they just named," he said.

"What? What did you say?" I asked him.

"You are our freshman candidate for Football Queen. Now get down there so all our class can see you," he told me.

Somehow, I managed to stand up and walk down the bleachers to the bottom of the gym. I heard voices yelling and cheering.

"We want Lori! We want Lori!"

I remember thinking, *They* have *been talking about me! They have been staring at me. Not because of my dad, but because they like me. They want me as a friend.* I suddenly could raise my head high and feel proud. I felt like my head would reach the top of the gym ceiling.

That was an incredible moment in my life—one that I can always turn to when I feel low or doubtful about anything.

My freshman class prepared all types of fundraising events to help raise money so that I might be the Football Queen of Pryor High School. Each penny we earned would count as one vote. Each freshman, sophomore, junior, and senior class was doing everything possible to gather the most votes for their class candidate.

Our first-year class came up with the most original ways to raise money, hoping that I could be crowned the Football Queen at the upcoming homecoming game.

Mom decided that I had to have a unique dress for the occasion, but after searching in all the local stores, she did not find what she had in mind for me to wear.

"Lori, I think we will have to plan a trip to Tulsa to shop for your dress, and I can visit your dad. You could also try contacting your friend Marc while we are there," she said.

That idea sounded great to me. I was very anxious to see if Marc was still around. I felt he would not have much to say to me, but the thought of maybe getting to see him made me happy.

Mom planned the trip for Saturday, and as we reached the outskirts of Tulsa, my stomach felt that familiar butterfly feeling I would always get when I would be around Marc. I know Mom could see that I was getting excited, so she found a place that had a phone booth and said, "Go on, call him! You will not be any good at shopping until you do."

I had always kept his phone number in my address book and had it with me.

I also had his Boy Scout ring in my pocket that I knew I needed to give back to him. It was not right for me to have it since we no longer lived near each other and couldn't date, and I knew that ring was special to him.

I nervously dialed his number.

"Hello," Marc answered.

My knees went weak, and nothing seemed to come out of my throat just from hearing his voice.

"Hi Marc, this is Lori. How are you?" I asked him. I fully expected him to say, *Lori who?*

"Hi, I am fine. How are you?" Marc answered.

After a few brief moments of silence, I collected myself and said, "Nervous, Marc, that's how! I was not sure you would remember me."

"Don't be silly; of course I remember you. Where are you? Where have you been?" he asked me.

"I'm here in town with Mom. She's going to visit Dad, and then we will go shopping." I was hesitant to mention Dad, but I needed to know what his reaction would be.

A few seconds passed, and he said, "How is your dad? I read what happened to him in the paper, and I know that is why you and your family suddenly left town. Why didn't you at least call me or let me know where you were going before you left?"

"I did call you, Marc. I called twice and told your mother I needed to let you know where we were going," I told him.

The silence on the other end of the phone was unbearable.

"How long will you be in town?" he asked.

"We are driving back this evening after shopping," I told him.

"I work today from 2 to 5 p.m. at the Chuck Wagon Hamburger Stand just below my street. See if your mom will bring you there before you all leave town. I want to get your address to write to you, and I want to see you," he told me.

"Okay, Marc, I would like to see you also. I'm sure Mom will bring me by," I said. I hoped that the excitement in my voice did not scare him away.

"See you then," he said as he hung up.

That morning seemed to last forever, and my nerves were a mess by the time we reached the Chuck Wagon that afternoon. Mom had visited Dad, then we shopped and found a beautiful dress for me to wear for the crowning of the Football Queen. Now it was time for us to see Marc.

As we drove up to the front of the Chuck Wagon and Mom parked the car, I sat with her, watching him through the front window.

"Well, are you going in? Or are you just going to sit here?" Mom teased me.

"I'm going, Mom, I'm going!"

As I entered the main door, I walked back to where he was cooking. He quickly glanced up at me from behind the grill, slowly took the hamburger spatula he held, and flipped over the meat he was cooking.

"Hi," he said as he smashed flat the hamburger patty he was cooking. The sizzling sound of that meat cooking seemed to echo off the walls.

"Hi, Marc," was all I could say.

"You look good, Lori," was his reply.

I thought to myself, How could he possibly know that? He had not taken his eyes off that hamburger patty he was cooking to death long enough to know how I looked.

"So do you, Marc," I answered. "I have the address you want."

"Good! Do you live very far from here?" he asked.

"Yes, it is about seventy-five miles from here, in the small town of Pryor," I told him.

"Really?" he answered. "That is not too far. I have an aunt and uncle that live there."

Not far! It was at the end of the world and thousands of miles away from him as far as I was concerned.

"Then maybe you can visit them, and you and I could see each other," I said.

"Maybe," was his answer. "How is school?"

"It is fine, and I like it!" I told him. I didn't tell him I was running for Football Queen. It didn't feel that important at that moment.

He had managed to flop four more pieces of overcooked hamburger meat over on the grill, and they seemed to have his complete attention. I suddenly realized the Chuck Wagon was full of people. I felt like a complete idiot. To me, no one was there but Marc, myself, and those pieces of meat.

Marc walked around to the edge of the grill, and without removing his eyes or hands from the cooking he was doing, he leaned forward and said, "Stick your address in my pocket and make sure it will not slip out."

"Okay, Marc. I would like very much to hear from you." I stood there with my hand in his pocket for a moment and carefully slipped him my new address along with his Boy Scout ring. I waited for a few seconds for anything he might say or do, hoping he didn't notice the ring.

Then a smile crossed his face, and he looked deeply into my eyes. That was enough for me. Once again, I got lost in the darkness of his eyes!

"I will write to you soon, Lori," he said.

"Bye, Marc. I sure hope so," I told him.

As I closed the door behind me and walked out of the Chuck Wagon, I floated out to the car where Mom was waiting, and I turned and waved at him, wondering how or when I might ever see him again.

I came out of my trance about five miles down the road when Mom said, "I could see you both from the car. Did he even look up from his cooking? How can you be so excited over someone like that?"

"Oh, Mom, you just don't understand," I told her.

A smile crossed her face, and for a moment, I thought, well, maybe she does!

My freshman class did not raise enough money, so I did not win. The winner was the senior class and their candidate, Pat Snoud. She was the new Football Queen. I did come in second, so I would be part of the ceremony.

Our class was just a few votes short of winning. But the honor I felt standing on that platform was enough for me. It was so exciting to have people around me who seemed to care and like me.

I felt pretty and exceptional when I stood there the night of the ceremony as they crowned Pat the new Football Queen. I was wearing the beautiful dress Mom had bought me the day we went to Tulsa, and I was happy.

Our classmates surrounded us while the two of us stood on the altar in the middle of the football field, and our band played our school song as they marched onto the field. I felt so grateful for Jeff and Jim getting me elected. I felt loved and respected, and it was beautiful.

Following behind Pat and her special escort, Jeff and Jim escorted me to the convertible that was there to drive our new Football Queen and me around the football track. The driver then slowly took us around the stadium several times as Pat and I waved and threw kisses to all the faces in the stands.

Almost every freshman football player waltzed me across the dance floor at the big dance held after the game. Boys I had never seen before asked me out for a date. Tonight was my special night—my time to shine.

As I lay in bed later, exhausted, sleep would not come. All those beautiful things that had just happened to me should be the only things on my mind, but they weren't. When I closed my eyes, I saw Marc, his dark eyes, and his smile, and I was hoping he was not upset about me returning his ring.

I also hoped, more than anything, that he would be able to convince his parents to come to Pryor to visit his aunt and uncle so we could see each other again.

CHAPTER 24

Adjustments for Terrell

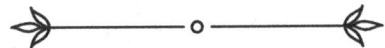

It was hard on us when Judge Olson sent Dad to jail and we had to move out to the country in Pryor. We all had to make a lot of adjustments. None of us were happy about the move.

Mom had to go to work, so it would be up to Granny to take care of things at home during the day. Mom felt that her mom could handle almost every change life would bring her. Mom worried about Terrell and me, but she felt the twins were so young that they would not have any problems with the changes happening in their lives.

Terrell began showing problems soon. He was too young to have his dad taken away from him suddenly, so he began to rebel. He felt hurt and alone. The only way he found he could handle things was to hurt back.

At the age of ten, Terrell needed his father. We were so wrapped up in our worlds that we didn't realize the effect losing his father was having on him.

Granny needed to give most of her attention to the twins because they were only seven years old. Mom was tired from working all day, but when she was at home, she would spend as much time as possible with them.

Mom struggled to keep us together as a family and keep food on the table for her four children and her mother.

Most of the time, Terrell was left alone to deal with his day-to-day issues. Terrell tried very hard to understand why his dad was gone and why all of us suddenly were taken away from everything and everyone we knew.

One of the issues that he had to deal with was food! Terrell could not understand why it was not as plentiful as it had been. Why couldn't he have what he wanted when he wanted it?

At first, it was just simple things he would do to get attention. When they stopped working, he found other things to do that would make us focus on him.

Terrell was strong and large for his age, and he was more than Granny could handle. His rebellion started taking over as meanness. He did everything he could to keep things in constant turmoil.

He took toys that belonged to the twins and broke them just for meanness. Food Granny would make us for supper, he would slip out of the kitchen and eat or feed it to Randy, our dog. When no one was looking, Terrell would dump out the buckets of water I had to pump from our well for Granny to use. He managed to do anything possible to make things more complicated for us.

"Terrell, I'll spank you with the strap if you don't behave," Granny would tell him.

But she could never catch him, and if she did, she would not be able to hold him long enough to spank him.

"Grab his legs," she would tell me when she needed to spank him, but he would always kick free from me and run and hide.

When Granny and I tried to tell Mom how Terrell acted during the day while she was at work, she would say to us that we were exaggerating. Terrell was smart enough to be on his best behavior when Mom was around, so she did not understand what we were trying to tell her.

Mom decided when we had to move from our home in Tulsa that we should bring some of our chickens with us. If we did, we would be able to have fresh eggs to eat, and we could also raise some of the chickens for eating.

One weekend, Terrell picked just the right time when Mom was home to get everyone's attention. It was a Saturday afternoon, and we were all busy with our chores—too busy to pay attention to him. I had just hung some laundry that Granny had finished along the fence line to dry when I noticed Granny walking down the path to the outhouse. She had just been there long enough to close the door, raise her dress, and position herself firmly on the one-holer when the door flew open, and she ran out screaming Mom's name.

"Adella, come quick, hurry!" she screamed as she struggled to get her clothes in some order.

I thought a snake must have bitten her, so I ran to her as fast as possible.

"Granny, Granny, what's wrong?" I asked her.

"Look down there, and you'll see what's wrong!" she pointed into that smelly black one-holer outhouse.

Well, I certainly was not excited to do that!

"Go on, Lori, look!" she repeated.

I stepped inside the outhouse, leaned over the hole carefully, trying not to breathe, and slowly looked down. Chickens were flopping their wings, climbing on top of each other. They were frantic, trying to fly up and out to freedom! The more they struggled, the deeper they would sink. Chicken heads were straining upward to survive, and strange sounds were coming from their throats. When Mom got there and saw what was going on, she determined we had to try to save as many chickens as possible.

Mom saw Terrell watching, so she grabbed him and told him to start digging the chickens out of the hole. She then stationed herself next to him. She took the chickens from him as he pulled them up to safety and then handed them to Granny to wipe them off the best she could with the apron she had on around her waist.

Then it was my job to dip them into one of the buckets of water I had drawn from the well to wash them off. After they were all out of that terrible hole and the mess was cleaned off of them, Mom gave Terrell another job. It was his job now to dry them off the best he could with the towel she provided him and return them to the chicken coop.

Mom was sure it had been Terrell that put them down in that smelly hole, so she waited for the right time later that evening to talk to him about it. She wanted to know why he would do such a terrible thing,

He did confess to her that he was guilty. He told Mom he did it to get attention, and it had worked!

We all felt Terrell had learned a harsh lesson by doing what he had done. And we were all glad that he seemed to have realized that was not how he should behave.

After that day, we all tried hard to make sure we paid more attention to him and wanted to show him that we did love him very much. We tried to explain to him that life would not always be as hard as it was right now, that soon Dad would be back with us, and we would all be together again. He would get his dad back one day.

It had been a few weeks since the chicken ordeal, but with all the attention now being on me, my new dress, and the Football Queen contest, Terrell once again was not the center of attention he wanted to be. Everyone was paying too much attention to me, his sister, and he was not happy.

The weekend after the Football Queen contest ended, Granny fixed us a special supper. We had hot dogs and her particular mac and cheese that she liked to prepare for us. Terrell wanted more than one hot dog, but Granny told him no. That did not sit well with him at all.

Later that night, when everyone was in bed, he decided to go to the icebox and get the stuff he needed to make a hot dog. He then found a few matches in the kitchen drawer and slipped them into his pocket. Cooking one hot dog was not going to be difficult, he told himself. Mom was already in bed, and he knew that Granny, the twins, and I were almost asleep.

It was time for him to get his revenge! Everyone had paid too much attention to me, and Granny would not allow him to have a second hot dog. He knew if he was careful, he could slip out, go to the barn, fix himself a second hot dog, and be back before anyone even missed him.

It didn't take him long to build a fire. The small stack of hay he piled carefully in the corner of the barn burned almost as fast as he had lit the match. Large flames started quickly and were already reaching the top of the barn. Before he knew it, the fire was out of control. He panicked and ran toward our house as fast as he could.

The size of the flames and the fire had started so fast it scared him. He was frightened and crying as he entered the house, yelling.

"HELP! HELP!"

Granny and Mom heard his screaming and went to him as he came running through the door.

"Terrell, what is wrong?" Mom asked him as she shook him.

"Mama, I'm sorry," he was screaming at her. "Mama, I was hungry and was trying to cook one of the weenies Granny would not let me have at supper. I didn't mean to start a big fire!"

By then, we could see the barn flames from the house.

"I've got to go get some help," Mom told Granny. "Wake the twins and get them ready to leave if the fire starts this way."

Mom drove as fast as possible to the nearest house and asked them to call the closest fire department. When the Pryor Fire Department reached our home, the barn and acres of wheat fields and farmland were already on fire and destroyed.

No one but our family knew the reason behind that fire. It was the most significant fire that the county had ever had.

That evening, after things had calmed down and Mom was trying to relax, she realized the time had come to find Terrell some special help. She had to try to find a counselor who could help him.

CHAPTER 25

Mom Gets Tough

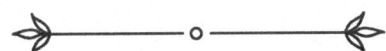

M om had to make a few decisions, and she knew it would be going against her husband's wishes. But the time had come for her to take matters into her own hands.

Her first step would be moving us into town, where we would have city water and more agreeable surroundings. The second step would be to seek counseling for Terrell. Her third step would be doing what she had to do to get her husband out of jail, so he could come home and take care of his four children.

Mom remembered reading in the Tulsa paper the day she had taken me shopping for my dress about the judge who had sentenced Dad to one year in jail for bootlegging. The article stated that the same judge had helped a man get released from his sentence to go home to take care of his hog farm. The report noted that his family was near poverty because the hogs in his care were dying. That was his family's total income, so the judge released him so he could go home and take care of his hogs properly.

So, with the same determination and guts Mom had possessed at sixteen, she took action on her decisions now. The first thing she did was to find us a small, friendly home in the city of Pryor and arranged to have us moved.

She then got Terrell into counseling, took a day off work, and drove straight to the Tulsa County Courthouse. She walked through the big doors, straight to the desk clerk, and said, "I'm here to see Judge Olsen."

The county desk clerk looked at her and told her, "I'm sorry, but he is tied up in court and won't be able to see you today. You need to make an appointment."

"Then I'll sit here until he gets out of court, or someone else in his office can talk to me," was Mom's reply.

"You may have a long wait, ma'am," the clerk told her.

"Well, that will be up to you! I'm not leaving here until I talk to someone," she told the clerk.

Mom then walked over to the long hallway that led to the main offices in the courthouse and sat firmly down on the floor. She leaned her head back against the wall, stretched out her legs, smoothed her dress carefully on each side of her legs, placed her hands on each other correctly in her lap, and closed her eyes.

The clerk walked over to her where she was sitting and said, "Excuse me, ma'am, You can't sit here. Please go to the front lobby and find a chair."

Without opening her eyes, Mom quietly replied to him, "You are wrong, my dear young man. I can wait right here. And I will still be here tomorrow night if that is what it takes."

Six hours later, Judge Olson finally agreed to talk to her.

Mom's argument with the judge was quite simple. She looked him straight in the eyes and said, "If you can let a man out of jail so he can go home and feed his hogs, you can damn sure let a man out to go home and feed and care for his four children."

Two weeks later, the judge released Dad and sent him home. One of the first things all of us noticed was the change in Terrell. The counselor had been right when he told Mom that all Terrell needed was a lot of love and attention and his dad back home. After just a few days of having Dad's attention and having him home, Terrell had become a new person. We were all happy to see the change it had made in him.

Dad's presence also made Mom much happier. But I still kept very distant and away from him when possible. I would never trust or love him as I had before.

I continued to keep to myself and stay in my world. My life had become much nicer since I had received a few short letters from Marc. That alone gave me hope, and I felt that someday, somehow, we would be together again.

CHAPTER 26

Another Move: Back to Tulsa

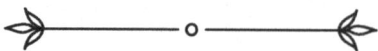

It took only about three weeks before Dad decided that he didn't care to live in the town of Pryor or the house where we lived. He told Mom that we were going to move back to Tulsa, and he would find work that he liked.

"We are moving back to Tulsa, Adella, and I don't want to hear any more about it," he told her.

"And just what am I supposed to do about my job?" Mom asked him.

"Quit!" was Dad's reply.

Mom then said to him, "How do you plan on supporting the kids and me? You have no real job training to do anything but sell whiskey. Where do you think you will go to work to take care of us?"

He started yelling at her, and we could hear the anger in his voice as he told her, "I don't know, but I'll find something, so you need to start packing."

Mom argued with him about it for days. She was happy with her nursing job, and she knew I loved the school I was attending. Mom told him repeatedly that we were all content and comfortable living where we were and didn't want to move back to Tulsa. In her mind, she felt and almost knew that Dad would get back into the same whiskey business if we did.

After a few weeks, she gave in to him, but she remembered how she always had let him take complete control of everything. She remembered when it all started. Dad had returned from the Navy, and she was working as a nurse.

She remembered that she had Terrell and me to care for at that time. Dr. Cook, who owned the local hospital in Okmulgee, had hired her and had fallen in love with her. Mom remembered that she had thought a lot of him and had finally agreed to divorce Edward once he returned to the States.

She remembered that Dr. Cook had helped pull her through a lot. She remembered that she had become very dependent on him to take care of her and her children without realizing it.

She also knew in her heart back then that Edward would never change. She felt that he would never get anywhere in the world. She knew that he was not concerned with their future as a family, only with what made him happy.

She remembered that her plans at that time were to better herself and the life of her children. Back then, it had only made sense for her to accept Dr. Cook's affection and care. She felt that she would put the divorce into action as soon as she saw Edward face to face.

She also remembered that she still loved Edward then and felt the only decent thing she could do would be to tell him in person. She thought she could not send him a letter to ask for a divorce while he was serving his country.

She also remembered that the minute she laid eyes on him, she couldn't do it. She always gave in to his charm and even gave in to his reason for running out on her the last time he told her they had to move from Okmulgee.

She had given in to him when he moved her children and her into that tent on the school grounds. She had given in to him when he pushed her again to move to that terrible small garage apartment that swayed when the wind blew.

She had given in to him when he told her he wanted more children and wanted her to stop working. She believed him when he told her they would make a lot of money if he became a bootlegger.

She always gave in to him, no matter what he asked, because she still loved him with all her heart. She knew all his faults, but her love for him always made her agree to whatever he asked her. To her, it was all worth it because she had him. So, after all the past years and four kids, she gave in to him again.

A few days later, Dad moved us all back to Tulsa. It took only three months for Dad to decide he could not stand things the way they were. He had tried working at selling vacuum cleaners, working as a delivery man for a cleaning company, and even driving a taxicab. None of these seem to be what he wanted to do.

One day, Dewayne Claremont, a past friend, ran into him and approached him about being a delivery man or a partner in his whiskey business. The offer was very tempting to Dad, but the time he had to spend in jail had been enough for him. Besides, Dad knew that if he returned to the whiskey business again, he would not be satisfied with being a glorified delivery man. He wanted to be in it at the top or not at all. Dad always felt he had to be the head of things, not the underdog.

Mom still was very important to him, and he loved her, so he knew he needed to keep the possibility of getting back into the whiskey business away from her. He knew she would leave him if he chose to get back in the whiskey business again.

He was very much aware that she was a strong-willed person. She had already proved that she could care for herself and their four children without him. This knowledge made him quite uncomfortable and strangely insecure about himself as a man. He wanted to be the one that ruled his kingdom. So, instead of being pleased with his wife, he had become very jealous of her.

During that same time, Dad became quite jealous of the young man who was now a big part of my life. He didn't like the idea that this young man had given me his Boy Scout ring or had asked me to be his steady girlfriend. A special boy in my life was not what he had planned for me. As far as he was concerned, his women were his and his alone.

Dad decided that day that the only way he could have complete control of his family would be to make sure we were somehow isolated from everything and everyone except him. He had to move us out of the city, away from interfering people. He had to regain control of all his children and his wife.

CHAPTER 27

Dad's Perfect Answer: Kellyville

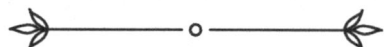

The perfect solution came to Dad when he ran into one of his old buddies, Roger Clements, while he was having a beer at one of the local beer joints in Tulsa. Roger owned a large ranch in the small town of Kellyville. Dad knew that Roger was the head of all the bootlegging businesses in Oklahoma.

Roger told Dad during their conversation that he had always had trouble keeping a ranch hand where he lived in Kellyville. He also told Dad that he didn't like paying them the money they seemed always to want. That seemed strange to Dad, as he knew that money was not an issue for Roger.

Dad felt that he and Roger had established a close relationship during those few beers, and he was going to use that friendship to get what he wanted if possible.

After drinking all the beer they wanted and having their long talk and a firm handshake, Roger invited Dad to see his ranch. He wanted him to come and look at the house he would provide for Dad and his family if he chose to be his new ranch hand and business partner. Roger told Dad it was not a very good house, and he may not want his family to live there.

Dad agreed to see it, and when he went there a few days later, he knew it was the perfect spot and where he wanted to move us.

The house was about thirteen miles out of town and set alone off a winding dirt road about three miles from the main ranch. It was in the middle of acres and acres of land. It was in terrible shape and well hidden by lots of trees.

Dad knew that he could repair it and make it livable for all of us, and his hands and body could use some hard labor.

While Dad and Roger stood there looking at the house, Dad said, "Tell you what, Roger. You provide me with the lumber, the tools, and some paint; I will get this place back in good shape for you. You no longer need a ranch hand since you only have a few cattle anymore, but you could use my help.

"After I fix it up and make it livable, I'll move my family here so I can help you. Then you, in return, can help me. You provide me this house, rent free, and enough money to keep food on the table to feed my family, and I'll keep the house and the ranch up for you. You owe this to me since I didn't give any information to the Tulsa police about your operation out here."

"Damn, Ed! I knew you wouldn't squeal on me, and the fact is, I think I would like to have you around," Roger replied. "We can go into town on Saturday nights, drink all the beer we want, and raise hell together. I'll help you and your family in any way I can. And I know my wife will be glad to have some kids nearby. How soon do you want to move in? Hell, I will even send a truck to move your family. I can also use some help managing all the whiskey business I have here in Oklahoma, along with support on the ranch."

A firm handshake was all the two needed to seal the agreement, and Dad now had what he had wanted all along.

Later that week, Dad drove to the ranch in Kellyville and met Roger. After hitting a few local bars in town and drinking as much beer as their bodies could consume, Roger took Dad to the ranch and showed him to his guest room. Dad fell asleep knowing he had made the perfect plan.

All he needed to do the next day was sober up, drive back to Tulsa, and tell Mom we would be moving again. Dad knew how to control her and knew she would agree.

Mom once more did what Dad asked her to do. It also meant that Granny would need to return to live with Uncle Chuck and Aunt Sue in Okmulgee and not with us.

Once again, we would need to make new changes in our lives and go to another school. Dad told Mom that the house he was moving us to had furniture, and it was small, so she needed to get rid of a lot of the things she had.

When Dad finished fixing up the house, he moved us. It was near the end of the school year, so we would only have a few weeks in our new school before summer would start.

None of us wanted to change schools again, but Mom took us and got us all enrolled. In Kellyville, there was only one school for everyone to attend. We found that we would all ride the same school bus, which would pick us up at the end of the dirt road that led from our house. The dirt road was about a block long, and none of us liked the walk we had to make to catch our bus.

Summer came after we'd spent only a few weeks at our new school. Most of that summer was spent with us just playing outside in the barn or reading whatever book we had.

When our school started again in the fall, we had at least three months before winter began. In the early weeks of December, almost five feet of snow had fallen on the ground. It was over two weeks before we could even go outdoors for any length of time. The school was closed, as no one could get to it.

The winter was hard and cold, and the black, ugly pot-bellied stove in the middle of our floor was all we had for warmth, and it was never enough. Even with extra layers of clothes on, the only comfort we could all get would be when we would climb in under the covers of our beds for extra warmth.

Mom sometimes would allow all four of us to climb into her bed because it was the biggest. That was when I loved reading to my brothers and sister.

The twins were now almost eight years old, and it wasn't easy to keep them entertained, but they did like crawling in bed for me to read to them. Terrell was not too fond of the idea, but he was cold and would finally give in and climb in with us.

Mom did what she could to keep herself busy. She always kept a fresh pot of hot potato soup on the stove for us. Dad usually went to the main ranch house to play cards with Roger and drink beer. He was always warm from the beer and warm from sitting near their large fireplace.

None of us could understand why Dad would spend most of his time at their home instead of with us. It was a harsh winter outside, and we were in a house away from everyone. We all felt the least he could do would be to stay with us instead of being gone all the time.

CHAPTER 28

Strange Visit

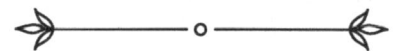

I remember the first and only time I visited the home of Mr. and Mrs. Clements since Dad had moved us into that old house and its isolated area.

Mrs. Clements had invited Mom over for lunch and asked her to bring all her children. She wanted to get acquainted with us because Mr. Clements thought so much of Dad. It was the middle of December and very cold.

All of us were seated and were waiting to be served lunch in her main dining area. Mrs. Clements had arranged for her maid to have the table set with beautiful china and crystal.

The table was covered with a beautiful lace table cloth. Matching napkins were carefully placed in napkin holders made from mother of pearl. A centerpiece of fresh-cut red roses surrounded by softly lit candles set in silver candle holders graced the middle of the table.

Mom was uncomfortable as soon as we entered the room. It was not a setting for two seven-year-olds. It wouldn't be easy for her to converse with Mrs. Clements because she would be too worried about the twins breaking something.

Mrs. Clements appeared to me as a very stately woman who seemed stern and unbending. But I did notice that when she smiled, the lines showed up at the edge of her lips and in the corner of her eyes, so this told me that maybe she was more pleasant than she appeared.

Somehow in just a few minutes, she made us all feel more at ease, and with the aid of Terrell and myself, Mom did have help keeping the twins controlled. Between the three of us, we could keep them from destroying the entire table setting and ruining our first beautiful lunch.

Mom wasted no time in letting Mrs. Clements know that she would like to take the twins and Terrell outside for a while as soon as we finished eating.

"Adella, please call me Betty. I want us to become friends. Will it be alright if I show Lori around the house while you take them outside? Then we can meet you in a little while and perhaps take the children to the stables for some riding," she said to Mom.

"That will be fine, Betty, but right now, I need to let the children get rid of some energy, or there will be nothing left of your beautiful dining room," Mom told her.

As the maid entered and started clearing away the beautiful china, Mrs. Clements said to me, "Lori, let me show you where I spend most of my time. It is my favorite place to relax, and I think you will enjoy it also."

She placed her arm around my shoulders and led me through the dining room, into the foyer, and up the winding stairway.

As she talked, I was busy taking in all the paintings throughout the house. They reminded me of the artwork I had been introduced to while on a school tour with my class and Marc not long ago when we lived in Tulsa. It was the Philbrook Museum, and it was full of beautiful artwork.

Mrs. Clements led me into what she said was her bedroom, telling me how lonely she felt and hoping I would become attached to this room, just as she was. *How can any person obtain this much splendor and still feel lonesome?* I asked myself as I stood there in total awe of the room and its beauty.

The walls, draperies, carpet, and bed coverings were soft blue hues touched with silver flakes that looked like silk. A velveteen chaise longue sat beside a massive four-poster bed made with wood that shined as if freshly polished. A fireplace filled the entire wall at the foot of her bed. The fireplace had been designed with matching squares of white stone that appeared to have flakes of gold mixed in. Placed carefully in front of the fireplace was a matching set of love seats covered in dark blue velveteen and two matching wingback chairs. Accessories scattered throughout the room were of fine-cut crystal and brass. A bouquet of fresh roses sat on a large glass coffee table.

Mrs. Clements removed a cigarette from a beautiful beaded case lying on the table, tapped the end several times on the back of her silver lighter, slowly drew in the flavor, and let the smoke release carefully from her lips into the air. Just as she did this, the fireplace crackled and hissed, and the fragrance of the wood filled the air.

I was standing at the edge of the bed when my knees seemed to weaken just from the total elegance of the room, and without thinking, I sat down only to realize what I had just done, and I stood up quickly and reached to smooth out the wrinkles I had made.

She laughed aloud, and her laughter seemed to bounce around the room.

"I can see you like this room almost as much as I do, Lori. I'm so glad! Go ahead and sit on my bed. This room is for pleasure, so don't be afraid of it or me. I want you to feel at home and comfortable here," she told me.

As she said this, she took one of the roses from the vase, walked over, and handed it to me.

"Did anyone ever tell you that you are a beautiful young lady?" she said.

My face blushed as I answered. "Thank you, Mrs. Clements, but anything would appear beautiful in this room," I said.

"Not so. If anything, it would appear out of place unless the object or the person was not beautiful. You seem to fit in this room quite well—as if you belonged," she replied.

Her hand was resting on my leg, and I could feel the warmth and strength of it through my wool skirt.

"Would you like to spend the night with me, Lori? I'll ask your mom for her permission if you think you would like to," she asked me.

"Where would I sleep?" I asked her.

"You seem to like this room so well, you could sleep here with me, and we could watch the fire and talk," she answered.

"But what about Mr. Clements? He would not want me here in his bed," I said.

She started rubbing my leg softly with her hand. "Mr. Clements and I don't share the same bed, Lori. He has his bedroom on the other wing of the house. I told you this room is for my pleasure, and it would please me very much if you would stay here with me tonight—and possibly many other nights, if you want."

Her hand was now only inches away from what I felt was a very private place, and I suddenly sensed the meaning of her words and actions.

I stood up and handed her back the rose. "Thank you, Mrs. Clements, for your offer, but I believe my mom will need me to help her with the twins. I'll think it over and let you know."

I walked quickly to the door, down what seemed to be an endless set of stairs, through the foyer, and finally outside into the fresh, clean air.

Later that night, when we returned home, I curled up in bed with my mom and the book *Little Women* in front of me. I knew that would be the only time I would ever want to revisit Mrs. Clements's house, but I tried to visualize her fireplace and bedroom, hoping it would help warm me up.

For some reason, my thoughts were all mingled with confusion, and my concentration on any one subject was just not obtainable. I began thinking again of the short time I had with Marc before Dad moved us one more time. By this time, I had already attended over five schools. During that time, Marc and I still managed to keep in touch.

I remembered when Marc had cared enough about me to ask me to be his steady girl when we were on Jan's birthday hayride. I remembered how he surprised me during that quiet time in the back of the truck by taking off his Boy Scout ring and placing it on my finger. I wondered how he felt when he found I had slipped his ring into his pocket along with my address in Pryor the last time I saw him at the Chuck Wagon in Tulsa.

He still, back then, had never done anything but hold my hand or put his arm around my shoulder. I always longed for him to pay more attention to me personally. I always wanted him to reach out and kiss me or pull me close to him so that I could feel the warmth of his body next to mine. But he never did. He never even tried.

Each time I would have to tell him goodbye again, he showed no emotion. He only said he would miss me but understood why I had to leave. "You have to go where your family goes. I will write to you once you tell me where you will be, and we will see each other again," he would tell me.

It seemed simple to him, but I would die inside every time we moved because I knew I would not be near him. He seemed to pass it off as though we meant nothing special to each other.

I began feeling sleepy after all those thoughts. I carefully placed my book on the end table. As I closed my eyes, I could only hope that maybe tomorrow would be a brighter day.

CHAPTER 29

Scary Eyes in the Darkness

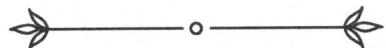

Sometime during the night, I woke in the room's darkness. I reached over to see if the twins were un-covered and carefully tucked them back in more securely. Had something disturbed my sleep?

I tried to adjust my eyes to the total darkness, listening, and I did hear something. Mom's breathing was easy, and I could hear soft snoring from Dad, yet I sensed something was wrong.

As my eyes slowly adjusted to the dark, I set up and looked around the room. Everything seemed normal, and then I turned my head toward the window beside our bed. Eyes—large sets of eyes—were close to the window. There must have been six or seven pairs of them looking straight at me. They were black as the night yet seemed to be glowing red.

"Mom! Mom!" I yelled.

Mom and Dad jumped up and came running.

"Lori, what in the world is wrong?" Dad asked.

"Look," I said and pointed to the window.

Mom and Dad just stood there staring back at the eyes for a moment. The eyes still had not moved. Those eyes were looking at us. By this time, Terrell and the twins were sitting in bed rubbing their eyes, wondering what was happening.

"Go back to sleep, everything will be alright," Mom told them.

Dad looked at me and said, "Lori, get on some warm clothes. You and I are going outside and scare those eyes away from this window and back to the barn."

"No, Dad, not me!"

"Young lady, do as I say!" he told me with that stern voice no one wanted to hear.

Mom nodded at me, which meant I should do as he said. I felt sure Mom wouldn't let me do anything she didn't think was safe, so I slipped out of bed, put on my coat over my pajamas, and then slipped on my boots.

The sets of eyes were beginning to move around, but they were still there, watching as Dad and I left to go outside. Dad opened the door to a cold blast of wind and pushed away the snow piled against the door frame.

The blackness of the night was lit only by the brutal stark whiteness of the snow. We bent our bodies against the wind and plunged slowly, step by step, through the deep snow that had already gone over my boot tops and inside to what only a few moments ago had been my warm feet. As we reached the back of the house, near the bedroom window, the eyes all turned to greet us.

During the blizzard that night, black Angus cattle had sought our house for shelter and warmth. They, too, were hoping for a better tomorrow. If I had not been so cold, I would have died laughing.

Dad and I worked together, slowly moving them toward the barn door. I was beginning to notice that my hands and feet were getting numb. They were feeling more like stumps hanging off my body with each step I took. It seemed like it took us forever to get those cattle in that barn, and I wondered if I would ever get warm again.

The results of that night sent me to bed for nearly three weeks with the worst case of flu I had ever experienced. Mom told me a few weeks later that my temperature had ranged from 103 to 105 for days. I had drifted in and out of consciousness, too weak to know or care what was happening to me. I was unaware of who was in the room or if anyone was even there.

My body knew it was lying in bed, but at times it seemed to slowly rise as if floating—drifting through the top of the house and into the clouds in the sky. I felt my skin falling off in chunks and tiny fragments as it floated up. Then all my flesh would be gone off my body. All that was left were just needle-thin bones, bones with no meat left on them, yet my brain remained in contact and kept working, thinking, wondering what was going on.

I could sense someone holding something that seemed to be going up and down. I could feel hands reaching and touching the area where my breast was supposed to be. I asked myself why anyone would want to touch something not there. I heard heavy breathing and could feel a face looking down at me. I floated off in a cloud, then darkness would come again, and I would rest and fall asleep.

I could hear voices in the distance fading in and out. "We must get Lori to a doctor or get someone to come out here. We have to do something."

"Mom, is that you?" I could hear myself asking. Yet I knew my mouth was not moving. How could it work if there was no flesh there for my lips? Why was all my skin falling off? My mind was not clear.

Then I felt the coolness of a rag and soft hands brushing my hair away from my face.

"Lori, Lori, honey, try and drink this. It will help you get better," Mom was saying.

My eyes opened, and I could see it was Mom beside me, holding a cup of warm broth from some potato soup. It smelled so good. I drank all of it without stopping.

"Oh, honey, I think you will be alright now," Mom said. She gently helped me lay my head back onto my pillow.

"Mom, what has been wrong with me?" I asked her.

"You have been a very sick girl, Lori, with a very high temperature. It took us three days to get it down to normal. Dad and I have been taking turns sitting with you," she told me.

"Mrs. Clements also came over and took the twins and Terrell to stay with her while I went into town to find a doctor so I could get you some strong medicine," Mom said.

"Who all was here while you were gone, Mom?" I asked her.

"Hush now, honey, and get some more sleep. I think you will rest much better now since you ate a little," Mom told me.

"My skin, Mom, is it still on me?" I asked.

"Yes, honey, your dad rubbed you with alcohol to help break your fever while I went to town to find a doctor. You will be alright now. Just get some more rest," Mom replied.

It was nearly a week before I could get up and stand on my feet. During my recovery, Mom would heat bricks on the coal stove in the kitchen area, wrap them in towels, and place them under the covers near my feet. She would then rub me down with Vicks ointment and make me breathe steam from hot water, which she would place under a newspaper tent.

As I lay in bed, I could watch through the window as the snow started melting. Spring was coming soon, and I hoped with all my heart that we would not be living in this place by the time the first robin made its appearance. I would lie there and watch Mom as she cooked, and she would come over and sit on my bed and bring me another bowl of her excellent soup.

"Mom, do we have to live here?" I asked her.

She waited a long time before she answered me. "You don't know how frightened I became while you lay here burning up with fever, Lori. It was then that I realized this was all so wrong. I have no right as a mother to subject my children to this type of life. I decided while you were lying there so sick that we will leave this place as soon as you are well and the weather warms up."

The twins and Terrell and I had only been there long enough to attend school in Kellyville for about four months. Mom was concerned about us changing schools all the time, but she was much more concerned about how and where we lived. She knew that things had to change, and they had to change fast!

Mom let me know that she had told Dad she would not subject us to the type of life he had chosen for us any longer. She told me that during one of her visits to Mrs. Clements's house to use her phone to call the doctor, she found out that Dad had been working with Mr. Clements in the whiskey business all this time.

Mom also told me that she had told Dad as soon as she saw him that evening that she found out about the whiskey business and was tired of us living in these conditions. She then told him he needed to pack his bags and leave! She did not want to see or hear from him until he found a decent job in a proper place and was there for at least a year.

Soon after Dad was gone, Mom made a phone call to Dr. Cook in Okmulgee. She knew that if she asked him for help, he would do all he could. After she explained to him what was happening in her life and where we were, he told her that he would send a moving truck to come and move her within the week.

He also told her not to worry about where we would move to or where she would go to work. He wanted her back at the hospital.

While Mom was at Mrs. Clements's home making that call, she told her that she had sent Dad packing and he was already gone. She also told Mrs. Clements that she did not let him have the car keys, so he had to walk wherever he went. Mom knew she needed the car to get us all out of that awful place.

It was only a matter of a few days when a large moving van came down that long dirt road and pulled up in front of our house to move us to Okmulgee. As soon as the movers had us packed and ready, Mom packed us into our car, and we were off on another adventure. As we followed the truck down the road, I didn't want to look back. I was so glad we were leaving that awful house in the wilderness.

CHAPTER 30

Edward: Finding His Way, 1953

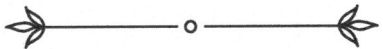

E dward had no idea whatsoever which direction he was going to go. He had not even bothered to tell Roger goodbye. Adella had told him to leave and that she didn't want to hear from him until he had a decent job somewhere for at least one year.

Adella could explain things to Roger however she wanted to. As far as he was concerned, Adella could handle the whole mess. He was pretty tired of the entire thing.

Walking down that long dirt road away from their home, he headed toward Route 66 near the edge of Kellyville. All he had was what Adella had packed for him in a tiny suitcase.

He would hitch a ride with whoever stopped first to pick him up. It took him almost one hour to reach the main highway and only a few short minutes before the first truck stopped.

"Where're you headed, buddy?" the rustic-looking old man hollered from the dirt-covered window of his truck.

"Whatever direction you are taking," was Edward's reply.

For weeks he drifted from one sleazy motel room to the next, from one town to the other, not knowing and not caring where he was, where he had been, or even who he was around. He repeatedly told himself that he didn't need to go to work to please anyone. He felt sure he could survive quite well, just as he had been living the past few weeks. He won an occasional poker game in some local bars in the towns he had passed through, which gave him pocket money. And someone was always ready to buy him a cold beer.

What else could he need or want? Using his charm on women or men was something that he loved to do. His appeal had always helped him get drinks or a bed where he could sleep. The women he met at the bars almost always provided him not only with good sex but a decent meal or two, so he was not concerned about his future.

He discovered he was enjoying life and the freedom of not having the responsibilities of a home and a wife and, most of all, the children who needed his discipline all the time. Edward knew without a doubt that he had handled his children quite well. They needed strict rules, and if they didn't follow those rules, he would always punish them somehow.

Adella was the one who had the problem of child management. She didn't understand that his way was the right way. After all, hadn't the firm discipline he had received from his father as a young boy been what had made him become a much better man?

He remembered when he was seven and his father discovered that he had stolen some gum from the corner drug store. His father dressed him in a frilly girl's dress for his punishment and told him that only sissies stole gum! He made Edward take some money to the store owner to pay for what he had taken. Then his dad took him back home, chained him up in their front yard where all his friends would see him dressed like a girl, and made him stay there all day.

He also remembered when his father caught him in the bathroom playing with himself. He made him drop his pants in front of his mother and tell her what he had done. He learned the hard way that he had to be careful with everything he did after that, because his father would punish him severely.

Things like that had made him a much better man as far as he was concerned, and this was what he wanted for his two sons. He couldn't help it if Adella did not understand his teaching method. Edward knew for sure that she would never understand what he had been teaching Lori, and as soon as his other daughter, Louise, was old enough, he would start teaching her.

In his mind, he knew it would help his girls become much better women if he was the one who taught them. He felt that their sexual training should come from him and him alone. He loved his two girls and wanted them to learn what sex was all about from someone who cared, not from some young boy who would be careless and maybe hurt one of them.

He felt entirely secure knowing that Lori would never tell her mother about what he had already taught her. At a very young age, the fear he had put into her mind about how her mother would think she was a bad girl and the fear of how unhappy the knowledge would make her mother feel was all that he knew he needed to tell her so she would to keep her mouth shut.

Edward also knew that Lori was very close to her mother, and for that reason alone, she would probably never say anything to her. He knew he had Lori convinced that it would bring her mother a lot of unhappiness if she told her what he had been doing.

He suspected Louise was going to be quite different. Teaching her would have to be handled differently, if he ever got that chance. Louise was only seven years old but was very independent and free-spirited. When she did grow up, Lousie would most likely be unable to keep her mouth shut about anything.

But tonight, he was not going to worry about any of these things. Tonight he was looking forward to his session in bed with his latest conquest he had met, and he knew it would be a good time.

He had hitched a ride to the big city of Houston, Texas. People he'd met told him that there the bars and women were plentiful. Today he would enjoy himself to the fullest in Houston, and maybe tomorrow, he would head to the beach he had heard of nearby in Galveston, where the gambling tables and the women were wide open.

His wife, Adella, could handle his children's problems back in Oklahoma. He was enjoying his life right now. He would contact her later, or maybe never.

A few months later, when he was still in Galveston, he kept hearing about a chemical plant hiring people and paying a good salary. Money was getting hard to come by, and he knew he needed to work for a while, so he headed toward the town of Freeport, Texas, to check the job situation. It didn't take long for him to get a job and move into a small trailer. He told himself that life would be easier this way, and he knew he wasn't getting any younger. Maybe it was time to settle down.

CHAPTER 31

Life without Dad

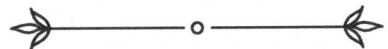

D r. Cook had promised Mom that he would have a perfect home ready and furnished for us to move into as soon as we arrived in Okmulgee. He gave Mom the address and told her it was just a block from the Okmulgee High School.

Dr. Cook knew the rest of our family well since they all lived in Okmulgee, so the first thing he did after talking to Mom was contact Granny to tell her what was happening. He knew Mom would want Granny to be there when we arrived at our new home. Both Granny and Dr. Cook were waiting for all of us when we drove up in the driveway.

Moving back to Okmulgee was the best thing that had happened to us in a long time. We were back happy and safe, and Dad was no longer with us or in control of our life.

Dr. Cook made life so much better for us, and we could not thank him enough. The best news he had for Mom was letting her know he had a job waiting for her at his hospital as soon as she got settled. He told her he would do anything for her if she let him.

I wasted no time getting myself enrolled in Okmulgee High School. It would be a few weeks before the school year started, and I was excited. I was going to be a sophomore that year. I also knew I would need to get my act together and buckle down after attending so many different schools.

My grades had been going downhill since changing schools so many times. It was because each school had different subjects and different ways of teaching. I knew I would depend heavily on my cousin Ellen to help me out since she was so smart. Ellen lived in the same place she had always lived and knew almost all the kids and teachers I would meet once school started. I hoped that she would help me over all the rough spots.

In the past, when we lived in the house that Uncle Chuck built for Granny, my cousin Ellen and I spent a lot of time together. She had not changed much since then except to be prettier. I found out that Ellen belonged to many notable school organizations. I knew she would help me join any of them if I wanted to. And we could go to each of them together.

When school started, that was the first thing she did. She introduced me to all her friends as her favorite cousin that had just moved here from the big city of Tulsa. After just a few weeks of going with her to some of those groups, it didn't take long to figure out that none were for me. Her friends and socializing were just not what I wanted or enjoyed.

In the afternoons when school was out, I would finish my chores at home, find a good book, and lose myself in the small loft at the top of our stairs. The loft was mainly for storage, but I had made myself a cozy corner for reading and being alone.

Sometimes late at night, after the twins and Terrell had gone to bed, the house would be quiet, and I would find myself slipping up there so I could read or write poetry.

I felt like I had so much to say and yet no one to share it with. Somehow putting words down on a piece of paper made things easier. Of course, most of my words and thoughts seemed to be about Marc and how I still felt about him deep down inside.

I still cared for Marc, yet I knew our relationship had ended. I knew I would not mail him the things I would write, but I wrote them anyway. It always made me feel closer to him if I could put down what I was feeling at the time.

Late one night, these words came to me while I was upstairs, and it was quiet.

IF

If you cared, as you once said you did

On that special hayride night,

We will be there for each other

When the time is right.

Until then, my love,

I will hold you silently,

In my heart

In the darkness of the night.

If we care for each other

As we said we did,

You will reach out to me

When you can.

I will be there, as always,

Someday—

Once again, when the time is right!

CHAPTER 32

Dating Others

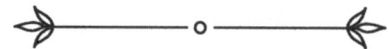

It was finally summer and school was out when I met Glenn Hook. It was a Saturday afternoon in the city park, and I was there with Donna, my new best friend. Donna and I had met at school in one of the classes I was taking, and we soon became good friends.

Donna and I discovered that we enjoyed each other and could have just as much fun as the socialites at school, only in a quieter way. Donna liked to bike ride through our local park, and so did I. We both wanted to be outside in the fresh air, with the sounds of nature around us. We didn't like having to dress up and act like socialites.

It was a beautiful Saturday morning, and Donna and I had finished our chores at home, so we decided to take a blanket and some of our favorite books to the park and stretch out under a giant shade tree. We were lying there reading and talking about the girls at school when two of the cutest boys walked up and started talking to us.

The spokesman for the two of them introduced himself as Glenn, but he didn't need to say anything as far as I was concerned. I got lost in his blue eyes and the dimple in his chin that moved when he spoke. The words he was saying didn't matter.

He asked if the two of them could sit with us and visit, and Donna and I agreed. They were both so darn cute!

After spending a few hours with Glenn and his buddy Don, we learned a little about each other.

Glenn asked me if I had a boyfriend, and I told him I did have someone special in my life, but he lived in Tulsa. Glenn then told me I needed to get over a boyfriend that lived far away and start having fun with him.

Donna and I learned during our talk that Glenn and Don lived in a small town about thirty miles from Okmulgee. They had graduated from high school the year before, and both worked in the oil fields for Glenn's father, who owned the company.

Donna and I soon learned that money was no problem for either of them, and it did not take long for us to know how to help them spend it.

Donna and I agreed to meet them at the park early each Saturday morning. We both knew our mothers wouldn't let us date boys that were older and already out of school, so we decided we would not tell them anything about Glenn and Don. They just knew that Donna and I were together and would spend the day doing what we wanted to do.

Most of the time when we were with them, our days would be spent together in the park or just riding around in Glenn's car. The four of us would do whatever we wanted to do. Sometimes they would take us to an afternoon movie or out to lunch. Then always took us back to the park to get our bikes so we could return home. We always told our moms the two of us were having fun, so they never questioned us about what we did during the day.

Glenn and Don sometimes would return to their hometown on weekends, or they would get a motel room and stay in Okmulgee. On Sunday afternoons, Donna and I would meet them again at the park and spend the rest of the day doing whatever sounded like fun.

Glenn was fun to be with, he made me laugh, and I felt happy when I was with him. He couldn't do enough for me, and I felt the same about him. I wanted to take him home and introduce him to Mom and Granny, but I knew they would disapprove. I was too happy and having too much fun with him to mess things up by doing that.

One Saturday when the four of us were riding around town, Glenn told me he wanted to spend some time with me alone. He told me he would drive his car into town the following weekend so just the two of us could be together. He said that Don would have to drive his own car, and he and Donna would have to do something independently for a change.

"Glenn, I can't do it next Saturday," I told him.

"Just why not?" he asked.

"My mom has been after me to date the son of one of her friends for a long time, and I promised her I would. Mom and his mother arranged for the two of us to go on a church hayride next Saturday. I haven't told her anything about you, and she thinks it is strange that I'm not dating very much. She told me it's time she found me a steady boyfriend," I told him.

"Well, I am your steady boyfriend, and I think it is about time that we let her know. I don't want you dating other guys," he said.

"Glenn, I'll tell her about you, but not just yet. I'll go on this hayride Saturday, as Mom wants. I promise I'll tell her about you soon," I told him.

Glenn agreed to wait and let me tell Mom when I thought it would be the right time, but he wouldn't let things go until I told him what he wanted to know. He wanted me to tell him where we would be going on the hayride and when we would leave the church. He asked me to promise that I would not let this new boy get fresh with me.

"You silly goon, I'm not interested in anyone but you," I told him.

The blind date our moms had arranged was a delightful surprise. He was a senior in the school I attended, but I had never noticed him. He was very nice looking, and his name was Gary. He came to pick me up in his car about an hour before the hayride and drove us to the local root beer stand by our school to sit and talk.

"I thought we should try and get acquainted with each other a little before we climb up in the back of the hay wagon together," he said as we walked to the root beer stand.

As soon as we sat down, Gary ordered two large frosted cold mugs of root beer.

"I'm sorry my mom and yours pushed you into this blind date with me," I told him.

"Don't be sorry, Lori. I've noticed you at school several times, and I was pretty anxious when I found out who they wanted me to date," he answered.

I felt a blush cross my face and found that I didn't know what to say to him. A few moments of silence passed when he asked, "What do you do for fun?"

I was glad he gave me a few moments to compose myself. "My girlfriend Donna and I spend most of our weekends in the park. We both enjoy being outdoors," I said. I was going to tell him about Don and Glenn, but I decided not to mention them for some reason.

"So, you are an outdoor girl?" he questioned.

"Well, I guess you could say that. I enjoy being outside, just enjoying the breeze, sunshine, birds, and bees," I answered.

"You can learn a lot from the bees if you care to," he laughed. Then he asked, "Have you ever played golf?"

"No, I haven't. It seems silly to spend time knocking a ball from hole to hole and chasing after it," I told him.

"Some people may think so, Lori, but they are usually people who haven't played the game before. Why don't you let me take you out next Saturday morning and teach you just how much fun it is to knock that silly ball from hole to hole?" he said, smiling.

"Where do you play?" I asked him.

"My parents are members of the country club, and I play golf there. I can pick you up at about eight o'clock on Saturday morning, and we can play a few holes. Then I would like to take you to lunch. After lunch, I can take you home so you can change clothes before we go to the show and out for supper," he said.

"Hey, wait a minute, Gary, I haven't even told you I would play golf with you yet, let alone spend the entire day with you!"

He looked at me and smiled and said, "I have a feeling you will before the night is over. Now drink up, or we will be late for our hayride."

I liked something about the way he just took over. I didn't doubt for a moment that I would do whatever he asked of me because he did it gently.

The men from church had filled our hay wagon to the brim with fresh-smelling hay. The smell reminded me of the barn in Pryor. Four enormous horses were pulling the wagon. Couples were already filling the wagon, and the daylight was about gone.

I again remembered for a few moments the hayride I had gone on with Marc. I found my thoughts drifting, wondering how he was and if he thought of me, as I often did of him.

"Let's hop on the back end, Lori, so we can sit on the edge and hang our legs off," Gary said as he picked me up and set me firmly where he wanted me.

As everyone got comfortable and snuggled in place and wrapped around each other, a giant full moon came into view as if it were waiting for the right moment.

The horses snorted and were anxious to get moving. With a sudden lunge forward, we were off. The sudden movement forward threw me off balance, and for a moment, I thought I was going to fall off the back of the wagon.

"Hang on," Gary said as he grabbed me. "I don't want to lose you now that I have just found you!"

We had gone only a few miles when I noticed the blue '49 Buick that hung back just far enough so it would not be noticeable. But I saw it, and I knew who it was.

So that was why Glenn had insisted on me telling him where we were going and what time we would be leaving the church. He needed to know so he could follow me.

At first, it made me mad, and then I thought it was funny. I decided if Glenn wanted to be jealous, I would give him a reason to be jealous, but as it turned out, I didn't have to make the first move. Gary had already decided he wanted to kiss me, and he did.

He put his arm firmly around my back and cupped my face gently in his other hand. He then took my chin and tilted my face up toward the moonlight.

"You are beautiful in the moonlight glow," he told me.

He then kissed my eyelids, lingering slowly on each one to embrace each eyelash. I felt my heartbeat increase as I waited for him to reach my lips. Instead, he laid me carefully backward on the hay, then took my hands and kissed and caressed the inside of my palms.

He rose on one elbow and looked down at me, using his free hand to caress my face. It was my time to see how handsome he looked in the moonlight.

"That feels very nice, Gary. You seem to know what you are doing," I told him.

"I think perhaps you just bring out the beast in me," he whispered in my ear.

"A beast is not that gentle," I whispered back.

I then put my arms around his neck and pulled him down to me. He met my lips gently at first, teasing me.

"It's a good thing that this is a church hayride, and we have an audience, or I'm afraid you and I would be in trouble," he said with a gentle laugh.

I wondered how he would feel if he knew just how much of an audience we did have. Glenn was still following us.

The hayride was a two-hour trip winding slowly around the lake, down a few country roads, then back to the church where it all started.

Couples climbed off the wagon when we arrived at church and headed toward their cars. Some would be returning straight home, some would head for the root beer stand, and some would seek a more secluded spot to finish what they had worked themselves up to while buried in the hay.

Much to my surprise, Gary told me he was taking me straight home because he was losing total control.

While most of the others were getting into their cars, Glenn was getting out of his. He met us halfway when we were walking toward Gary's car. I had no idea that Glenn would carry things this far.

Glenn walked straight up to me and said, "It is about time you got back!"

He then took me by my elbow and started walking me toward his car.

"Wait a minute, Glenn," I said to him. I turned to Gary and said, "Gary, this is Glenn, a friend of mine."

"I'm more than a friend of hers," Glenn replied in a voice I had never heard.

"I think that should be Lori's choice, not yours," Gary said to him.

Glenn started pulling at my arm, insisting I go with him.

"Hey, wait a minute, I told you I had a date tonight. I'll see you and talk to you tomorrow. Tonight I'm out with Gary," I told him.

"Either you come with me now, or there will be no tomorrow for us," Glenn said to me in an angry voice.

After that statement, it didn't take long to make up my mind.

"That's fine with me, Glenn. If that's how you feel, then we have no tomorrow," I told him.

As Glenn stood there trying to figure out what to say next, Gary opened the car door, and I climbed in. Then he got in, started the engine, and leaned over and kissed me.

"I think you just made a wise decision, and I'll try to see to it that you won't regret it," he told me.

On our ride back home, I knew Gary was right. Glenn was too much like my dad. I remembered how he always wanted to control Mom, and I sure didn't need that!

CHAPTER 33

Saying Goodbye

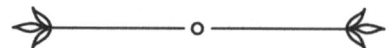

It was now summer, and school was out. Life was better for all of us since we no longer lived in Kellyville. A few months had passed since we had moved to Okmulgee, and a lot had happened in a short time.

The one thing I missed the most was my dog, Randy. Mom told me we lost him during that terrible snowstorm in Kellyville when I was so sick. He followed me when I was helping Dad get the cattle to the barn that night and never returned home.

I had been dating Gary for a while and had not seen Glenn since we drove off, leaving him standing in the driveway of our church. Gary had turned out to be an excellent choice for me, and he also made Mom very happy. She liked Gary very much.

After I chose not to see Glenn anymore, Donna and Don broke up. My friendship with Donna was never the same after that for some reason, so I found myself again spending a lot of time with my cousin Ellen.

Terrell's life had also changed. He had started playing touch football at school and had made many new friends. One evening, when I asked him how he was doing, he told me that he sometimes missed Dad.

"Why on earth would you want to see him again? All he ever did was mistreat you!" I asked him.

"Lori, all the boys at school have a father, and I don't. I miss that, that's all. It would be nice to have my dad at some of my games." he told me.

"You tell them you have a father, but he is a traveling salesman. You don't have to tell them another thing," I told him.

"Okay, Lori, I'll say that, but I still miss just having a dad," he said.

"Make friends and play the best football you can, Terrell. We are all there watching you, and you'll see him again. He and Mom have not divorced yet, so you still have a father," I explained.

I knew it would not make the hurt go away for him, but I hoped somehow it might give him something to hang onto. I also hoped—no, I prayed—that seeing Dad again would never take place.

The twins, Louise and Lee, were changing fast. They seemed always to be underfoot. Granny was happy taking care of them while Mom worked.

Granny seemed to always have a twinkle in her eyes. Somehow she still found the time to read stories from the Bible, only this time, the twins would be who she would read to the most, not Terrell and me.

I missed that part of my youth more than anything. I missed climbing into bed next to Granny and falling asleep with the sound of her voice reading the verses out of the Bible, and most of all, I missed the blinking on and off of my special red lights outside the window, saying *Lori, go to sleep, Lori go to sleep.*

Mom was busy working at the hospital to provide a living for us. We didn't have the fancy new clothes that some other kids had, and we did without many little extras other families seem to have, but we were all okay. We had a decent home, good food on the table, and a certain amount of freedom, along with a certain amount of discipline. It wasn't the strict laws forced on us when Dad lived with us, but it was discipline. Most of all, I was so happy not to have that fear of being alone with him anymore.

I often reminded myself of this when I would resent Mom never being at home like most mothers were. I also thought about what Dad had taught me to do with the boys I would date. I hated remembering those things and worked hard to bury them.

I struggled when I would find myself remembering what he had done to me and realizing how soiled I felt.

How could anyone ever want me if they knew the absolute truth about me? I had to make myself push all the ugly thoughts deep inside to feel better. I would tell myself that Dad had done everything to me because he loved me. I was unique to him. I was his princess.

I hoped that Mom would do what she should do, which would be to divorce Dad and marry Dr. Cook. But I knew for that to happen, Dr. Cook would have to divorce his wife.

It was evident that Dr. Cook and my Mom cared for each other. You could see it in their eyes when they talked to each other. He visited our house at least twice a week to see the twins, Terrell, Granny, and me. Sometimes he would sit quietly and talk to us, and sometimes he would join us for supper. He was always dressed in a suit as if he was going to or coming from a business meeting. I never felt comfortable around him, but he had been very kind to my mother, and I admired him for that. I often wondered if his wife was aware of his second family. I questioned Mom one night about her relationship with him. I felt she would tell me the truth.

"It may be hard for you to believe this, Lori, or even to accept or understand it, but Dr. Cook is nothing more to me than just a very dear friend. I care for and admire him, but it is not the same as what I felt for your dad. I hope you will understand that he is a wonderful man, and his wife is a dear person. I would never do anything that would ruin that relationship. Dr. Cook cares for you, Terrell, and the twins, and he will always help us any way he can, but that is as far as it will ever go," she told me.

Deep down, I didn't believe her, and I hoped that this time, just for once, Mom was not telling me the entire truth.

It was Saturday night, and Gary was coming to pick me up for what he said would be a memorable evening. I was excited but wondered what he had meant by that statement.

Granny noticed that I looked different for this date and said, "Lori, you look awful pretty tonight. Where is this special young man taking you? Sit here and let me help you with your hair." She pointed to Mom's dressing table.

"He is exceptional, Granny, and I like him a lot. He told me he was taking me to a show and then out for a drive. He said he has something special he wants to talk to me about," I told her.

I saw and loved the teasing twinkle in her eyes as she brushed through my hair and questioned me a little further. "Now, Lori, don't let this get too serious. You still have a few more years of school to attend. Didn't your young man graduate this year? What does he plan on doing with himself now?"

"I don't know, Granny. I haven't let myself think about it," I answered.

Terrell yelled at us from the front room, "Your date is here, so quit primping and come on out."

"Oh, Granny, sometimes I hate my little brother!" I told her.

As I got up to meet Gary, she laughed at me and gave me a big hug. "Terrell's not a bad kid like he used to be. He's just a boy and likes teasing his big sister. You run along now and have fun with your young man. I'm happy you have gotten over that other young man, Marc," she said.

It surprised me that she even remembered Marc's name, but I was even more astonished that she realized the hurt I had endured trying to get over him. I hugged her back, holding her just a little longer than usual. "Granny, I can't hide anything from you. I don't think I will ever get over Marc. I'll always miss him," I told her.

Granny hugged me a little tighter and said, "Lori, there is always another day, and who knows, maybe tomorrow you will see him again. No one ever forgets their first love, so you hang on to your thoughts of Marc and remember that each young man you meet will bring something unique to your life. When you get old like I am, you'll find those memories will help you get through each long day."

"I love you, Granny," I told her.

"I love you too, Lori. Now don't keep Gary waiting any longer," she said.

As I left the room, I noticed Granny taking out the hanky she always kept tucked in her bosom and used it to dab the corner of her eyes.

I was much quieter than usual on our date, and Gary sensed something was on my mind.

"What's going on with you tonight, Lori? I noticed you didn't seem to enjoy the movie," he said.

"I enjoyed it, Gary; I guess I'm just sorta moody tonight, and besides, something that Granny said to me earlier is bothering me," I told him.

"Do you want to talk about it?" he asked.

"Not just now, Gary. Maybe later," I told him. I had to stall my question for him just a little longer.

He drove us to the lake and our favorite parking spot, then turned off the motor.

"Let's get out and walk tonight, Lori, instead of staying in the car. I want to see you again in the moonlight like I did the first night we were on our hayride," he said.

We walked hand in hand until we found a flat rock that hung over the edge of the lake that we could sit on. The moon was beautiful, and the cricket sounds seemed to echo off the water as it rippled gently under our feet.

Gary sat behind me and encircled me with the gentleness of his arms. "Now tell me what your granny said to you that has you in such a quiet mood," he said softly in my ear.

"Granny asked me if I knew what you planned on doing now that you have graduated from school, and I have been afraid to ask because I think I already know the answer. I haven't allowed myself to think of you not being here, but I know you won't be. You're going away to college, aren't you?" I asked.

As I turned, put my arms around his neck, and looked into his eyes, I could see his answer.

He laid his head on my shoulder and clung tightly to me, trying to delay the next moment of unspoken words. I could feel the vibration of his voice against my chest as he finally answered.

"That's what I needed to talk to you about tonight and hopefully make you understand it's something that I have to do. But, I'll miss you so very, very much."

"Oh, Gary, I know you have to go. I am so proud of you! You want to be somebody important. Most boys don't care about the future, but you do. You have to go to college. I'll be here when you get out, and we can see each other on your breaks and during the summer," I told him.

"Lori, it wouldn't be fair of me to ask you to wait for me, but I want you to know that I will see you every chance I get, and that I love you!" he said.

"I love you too, Gary. Let's enjoy what little time we have left before you go, just being together," I answered.

He then laid me down gently beside him on the rock where we were sitting. The coolness and texture of it felt good through my sheer summer dress. I had always managed to keep any of the boys I had dated from going all the way with me, but tonight I felt it might be different. Tonight I had a lot of mixed emotions.

After a few moments of feeling the closeness of each other's bodies and knowing we would not see each other for quite a while, our desires became more intense.

I watched and waited while he took the protection out of his billfold and placed it on himself. It was strange that he turned his back to me so I couldn't watch. He then turned back, facing me, and said, "Lori, if I hurt you, please tell me, and I will stop."

"I will, Gary, I promise," I told him.

He kissed my face, neck, ears, and lips. I closed my eyes and waited for the sensation I was feeling to end, and when it did, I knew he must have reached his peak.

Gary rolled over on his side once again and lay quietly beside me. "Are you alright, Lori?" he asked as he looked at me.

"Yes, Gary, I'm okay," I told him.

He raised up on his elbow, looked down at me, and kissed me gently.

"You sure do make me feel good. I'm so lucky to have a girl like you in my life. Maybe I should stick around here and stay with you instead of going off to college," he said.

"Don't be silly; you know you have to go!" I replied.

After he took me home and we said our goodbyes that night, I lay in bed and asked myself why I took the chance of possibly getting pregnant. I knew I could have pleased and made him happy without letting him do what he did. Dad had told me more than once that all the kissing and petting you share is okay. It is for pleasure. He had told me repeatedly you can make a man happy in other ways. You should never let a man penetrate you with his body until you are married. But I knew the only thing that mattered to Gary and me that night was that we cared for each other and felt happy. What Dad had told me to do didn't seem right.

It was hard telling Gary goodbye that next evening when he came over. He was leaving and going to Harvard University, far from Okmulgee. I promised him before he left that I would write, and he, in turn, promised me he would do the same.

"Take care of yourself, Lori. You're so very special to me," he said.

As he waved goodbye, I gently tucked the memory of him away for when I got old as Granny had told me to do.

Gary had been gone for a few weeks when I added my thoughts of him and that particular night we had spent together to my diary.

GOODBYE

In the moonlight glow

I felt you

And for a few brief months

You were mine.

Now the future calls you

To another destiny

And you are gone,

Only to be a lasting memory

Tucked safely and lovingly

In the darkness of my mind.

CHAPTER 34

Adella's Special Phone Call

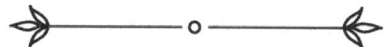

Adella had just come out of the nurse's lounge after a thirty-minute break. She loved her job as a nurse. She had no idea what each day would bring her, but she did the best she could. Today her feet and legs felt like they weighed a hundred pounds each. She knew she still had three more hours left on her shift, so she needed to shake off the hurt and concentrate on her patients.

She had scrubbed up at 6:30 that morning to assist Dr. Cook with the delivery of a baby. It was supposed to be an easy delivery, but it turned out different. It was a breech birth, and they almost lost the tiny baby girl.

At 10:45 a.m., a man came in needing emergency surgery. When the hospital assigned him to room 201, Adella went into his room with him.

Adella assured him that Dr. Cook would help him. The skill of his hands and the help of God would be all he needed. Adella could see that Mr. Sneed was distraught, so she tried to calm him by telling him he would be fine and back in his room, walking around, in five or six hours. It would be a simple removal of a cyst that had grown quite large on his back close to his spine.

"Mr. Sneed, you will be okay. It is an effortless operation. You could also be awake while Dr. Cook removes it. He can use a local anesthetic," she told him.

"Oh no, I don't want to know anything! I need you to know that I'm scared to death! Please make sure that you sedate me during surgery. I don't want to hear anything or watch anything. Is that understood?" he asked.

Later, Adella remembered her conversation with Mr. Sneed just before his surgery. She had once again assured him that he would be just fine. *Why didn't I realize then just how frightened he was?* she asked herself.

She had told him that she would make sure he was out entirely but had also told him he would be sorry because, she said with a smile, a good-looking nurse would be assisting during his surgery.

He had smiled at her when she tucked the sheet around him to make him feel more secure. He had taken her hand and patted it.

"You're a good nurse," he had told her. "You take time to talk to us silly old men, and that is nice for you to do that."

Adella remembered how his gentleness had touched her, yet she saw the fear in his eyes.

She thought to herself, *I wonder if I could have done more?* But it was too late now.

Mr. Sneed died on the operating table at 1:32 p.m. The operation was over, and they were preparing to take him to intensive care for a few hours for observation. The anesthetic was beginning to wear off, as they had only given him a small dose. He had opened his eyes long enough to realize where he was and suddenly entered cardiac arrest. There was nothing Dr. Cook or his assistant could do to revive him. Mr. Sneed had died from simple fright.

Adella tried to regain her composure as she returned to regular duty when Helen, one of the floor nurses, told her she had a long-distance phone call. She then told Adella that she was sorry to hear about Mr. Sneed.

"No one would ever think that something like that could happen so quickly," Helen said to Adella. "We all know you did the best you could do."

As Adella went to answer the phone call, she tried to shake the thought away that maybe she could have prevented his death. She knew how frightened he had been of having surgery.

"Thank you, Helen. Did they tell you who it was that was calling?" Adella asked.

"No, he just said he wanted to speak to Adella," Helen told her.

"Hello, may I help you?" Adella said after she picked up the phone.

After a few moments of silence from on the other end of the line, she started to hang up. "I think you are probably the only one in the world that can help me!" the voice on the other end finally said.

She was stunned. She had not heard from her husband since she had sent him away almost a year ago. "Ed, is that you? Where are you—are you alright? How did you know how to reach me?" she asked him in a shocked voice.

"I'm no fool, Adella. I knew who you would run to when you needed help. How is that jackass anyway?" he said.

She was so angry with him for saying that, that she almost hung up on him.

"If that's you called about, the answer is he's just fine! But I would think you might ask how your four children are. That jackass you referred to has seen to it that I have been able to put food on the table for them. That's more than I can say about you as their father," she answered quickly with anger.

"Hell, Adella, you're the one who ran me off, or have you forgotten?" he asked.

"No, I've not forgotten! Do you have a decent job yet?" she said.

"Well, as a matter of fact, I do. I live and work at a new chemical company close to the Gulf Coast in Texas. I thought maybe you and the kids might be ready to join me," he told her.

"And just how long have you had this job, Edward? Two weeks, or maybe even three?" she answered.

There was a short moment of silence before he answered. He could feel the bitterness in Adella's voice and knew this wouldn't be an easy conversation. "I've been here six months, Adella, and I like it a lot. I know it's hard for you to believe me, but I miss you and the kids. How are they?" he asked her.

She hated herself for loving this man. Her thoughts told her to ask him for a divorce and say she didn't want to return to his type of life again. She knew she needed to tell him she wanted out, but her reply said something different.

"The kids are all doing well. Terrell has been playing touch football at school. He's the one that seems to miss you the most," she said.

"Adella, why don't you let him come down during the summer and spend some time with me? I live close to the beach, and we could spend some time together fishing," he told her.

"And just who would be watching him during the day while you are at work? It's not that easy. I can't just up and let him be with you when I know nothing about your living conditions," was her quick answer.

"Damn, Adella, I'm his father, and he is almost twelve years old! Terrell can take of himself a few hours a day while I'm at work," he said.

"I'll have to give it a lot of thought, Edward, before I say yes to you about anything. Please write me a letter and send it here to the hospital. I'll decide after I've heard more from you," she told him.

"You mean you can't even give me your house address? You know I can find it out if I want to," he answered.

"If you are truly interested in your family, you can do a lot, Edward. It's all up to you!" was her answer.

"Okay, Adella, have it your way. But, for now, you'll be hearing from me again soon, that I can promise," he told her.

"You have promised too many things to me before, promises that you never kept. You'll have to prove yourself to me before I am ready to believe in you again," was Adella's reply.

When she hung up the phone, she knew it would only be a matter of time before she would say yes to him again. The fast pounding of her heart confirmed what she knew all along. She still loved him very much.

As Edward heard the click on the other end of the phone and it went dead, he knew that no matter what it took, he would win her back. He wanted his family, but most of all, he wanted her!

He had reached the bottom of his journey and was now climbing back to face life again. He had discovered at the bottom of his hell pit of life that Adella and his children were the only ones who mattered to him.

After a few weeks of giving the idea much thought, she knew she had to arrange for Terrell to spend some time with his dad. She would have to provide Edward with the chance to show her that he had changed and could be the man she had always wanted him to be.

But first, she needed to drive to Tulsa and visit her brother Doug. He knew more than anyone other than Granny what she had been through, and she trusted her brother's advice.

She also needed to talk to Terrell and Lori to let them know what was on her mind, and she would do that on the way to Tulsa.

CHAPTER 35

Lori's Phone Call to Marc

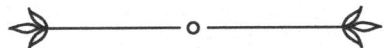

The next day, I woke up hearing Mom in the hallway outside my bedroom crowing like a rooster. Terrell and I knew that was a sign that Mom wanted us up and that she was in a good mood.

Her screeching imitation of a rooster was a horrifying way to wake us all up from a deep sleep but, by the same token, rather funny. As I lay there covering my head with my pillow, I vowed that I would never wake my children up like that. It was one family tradition I had no intention of ever carrying on. I stretched my legs and used what energy I had that early in the morning to swing myself up and into a sitting position on the side of my bed. The morning sunlight was shooting eerie rays of sunbeams across my bedroom wall.

Mom tapped on my door a few times before she entered. "Good morning. It's time to get up, Lori!"

"Mom, did you kill that rooster crowing outside my door? He sounds sick. Or did you try and revive him like the one we had when we lived in Tulsa?" I asked her, laughing.

Mom laughed back at me, and from the look I saw in her eyes, she did feel good this morning.

"What is the big occasion? Are you off today?" I asked her.

"Yes, I am, Lori. I have a few days off, and I thought we might take a little trip," she told me.

"A trip where?" I asked.

"Well, I thought you, Terrell, and I would drive to Tulsa and spend the night with Uncle Doug and Aunt Beth. I haven't seen my brother in quite a while," she said as she pulled me up on my feet.

"I like Uncle Doug and Aunt Beth. I would love to see them again," I told her.

"Good. I know you and Terrell always liked the park in Tulsa, so we might pack a picnic lunch and make a day of it. Granny will stay here and take care of the twins, so the three of us can spend some time together. Now pack up some overnight clothes, and I'll start us some breakfast and get Terrell up," Mom told me.

As she left the room, I knew it would be good for Mom to get away from work. She needed to just relax for a while. But I was also wondering why she seemed to be so happy.

When I started digging through my dresser to find what I needed to take with me, I ran across my old address book tucked carefully under a pile of nightclothes. Was it just coincidental that the page opened as it did?

Marc Lucus, 607 Lyndell. Phone 499-7591. Tulsa, Oklahoma. I closed it carefully and placed it along with my nightgown and a change of clothes in my suitcase. Maybe I would call him, and maybe I wouldn't. Who knew?

Mom outdid herself with breakfast that morning. We had eggs, ham, biscuits, and gravy. I loved sitting with her at the breakfast table and enjoying a breakfast she had found time to prepare. Mom indeed was not herself this morning.

Secretly, I made another vow to myself that morning. I would never work as long as I had small children at home to raise. I told myself I would be home to cook for them and enjoy them, just as my mother seemed to be doing for

Terrell and me on this rare morning. I knew she had to work to feed us. But, if possible, I would see to it that I married someone who wouldn't need me to work.

Our trip to Tulsa was enjoyable, and it was fun playing all those silly games with Terrell that you play when riding in a car. We each got one point for every white horse we spotted, but it would make Terrell mad if I spotted one first. So I started a different game that was not a contest. We had to read the billboard signs on the highway and then add the phrase "between the sheets." This game was fun, and even Mom joined in with us. We also had the Burma Shave signs to read every hundred feet or so along the highway. That helped us pass the time while we drove to Tulsa. When we finally arrived at Uncle Doug and Aunt Beth's home, they were their usual bubbly selves. They always made us feel very warm and welcome.

I had forgotten how much my mom and Uncle Doug looked alike, even though he was a few years older than her. I had also forgotten that he had the same twinkle in his eyes that Granny had when she was in a teasing mood.

Aunt Beth was still a pack rat. I was always amazed at the number of things she kept tucked away. She had two or three of everything, as if she feared she could never replace them.

One thing was for sure: you never went hungry when you were at their home. Aunt Beth could open a cafeteria and feed people without going to the grocery store for weeks. She had two freezers in her garage, plus the one she had in the kitchen crammed full.

She would tell us to help ourselves to anything we wanted, especially any of the ice cream, cookies, or candy she had everywhere. All these were luxuries for Terrell and me. Mom was able to keep us fed but could not provide all the extra goodies we always found at Aunt Beth's house. I remember even finding packages of food and candy in her bathroom medicine cabinets.

That evening we just spent time listening to each other's stories about what had been happening in our lives since we had last seen each other. Uncle

Doug brought out some old pictures he had taken when we lived in Tulsa and saw each other a lot.

He loved telling stories of the past. Aunt Beth handed me a photo and said, "Here is one I took of you and that young boy Marc when you were both standing in front of your dad's old stock car. Do you remember?"

The picture of Marc and me standing there side by side made me very glad I had brought along his phone number. I knew I had to call him after seeing that photo.

"Yes, Aunt Beth, I remember it. Will you let me keep this one? I don't have any of us together," I replied.

"Honey, of course you can have it," she told me.

I left the room to put the picture in my suitcase, and as I sat on the bed holding the photograph in one hand and my address book in the other, I was working on the courage to call him. It had been almost one and a half years since I last talked to him, yet in a way, it felt to me as if it had not been any time at all. I still felt as close to him as if we had never been apart. *It all seemed so silly!* I told myself. *Call him, and find out how he is.*

It had been a long time, and I was hesitant, but I had to do it. So I picked up the phone and dialed his number. When he answered, his voice was deeper yet softer than I remembered, and I thought it was someone else for a moment.

"Hi Marc, this is one of your long-lost girlfriends calling to see how you are." I hated it the moment I said it!

"Which long-lost girlfriend?" he answered.

"What do you mean, which one? How many long-lost girlfriends do you have?" I teased him.

"How many should I have?" he answered.

"I was hoping for only one! It's me, Lori."

"I know who you are, Lori. I'm just teasing you," he answered.

"You shouldn't do that, Marc!"

"Why?"

"Because you hurt a girl's pride that way!"

"Why?" he said again!

"Well, because no one likes to feel like they are just a string of many," I told him.

"Why?" he once again replied!

"Marc, quit saying 'why' all the time! Tell me how you have been."

"Why?" he again repeated.

"Marc, I will hang up on you if you don't quit," I said.

"Why?" Then he laughed. "Where are you?" he asked me.

"I'm at Uncle Doug's house. We will be here a few days." I told him.

"Just a few days?"

"Yes, Marc. We are going back to Okmulgee on Monday morning."

"Why Okmulgee? Do you live in Okmulgee now? I thought you still lived in Kellyville."

I realized then that he hadn't received the letters I wrote to him each time we moved. I felt his mother was still making sure he didn't get any mail from me.

"I would like to see you, Marc. Do you think we can get together maybe tomorrow evening for a while?" I asked him.

"Do your Aunt and Uncle still live in the same place?" he asked.

"Yes, they do."

"Then how about I pick you up around three tomorrow afternoon. I can use my dad's car, and we can drive out to the park, and I can have you back by six."

My heart was pounding so hard. I hoped Marc could not hear it. "That would be great, Marc. I will see you then," I told him.

"Why?" once again was his silly reply.

"Oh, silly, don't start that again," I told him.

"Okay, Lori, I'll see you tomorrow at three."

It was as if the past time did not exist. To me, it felt like the day after the hayride when he had given me his Boy Scout ring and asked me to go steady.

Mom could tell I was bubbly about something as I walked back into the living room.

"Who were you on the phone with, honey?" she asked me.

The teasing smile on her face told me she knew I had been talking to Marc. Marc had always been one of her favorites.

"Mom, it was Marc. He wants to take me to the park tomorrow around three if that will be alright with you. He said we would be back by six."

"Of course it will be alright, Lori. It will be nice for you to see each other again. I'm glad you called him," Mom said.

The next morning while I was waiting for three o'clock to come seemed to last a lifetime.

After he picked me up and drove us to the park, we walked around a while, and it didn't take long for me to see that nothing had changed about him. He still didn't have much to say (other than that teasing "why").

He did hold my hand while we walked, but he still made no move to show any extra affection or emotion toward me. He told me he would like for us to keep in touch and would like to have my current address and phone number. He told me that he had missed me and always wondered where

I was, but he figured that I had forgotten about him with all the moving around my family did.

I asked him if he had a steady girlfriend and how he was doing in school. He told me he just dated different girls but had no one special. He told me he still worked at the same hamburger place and mowed yards for people.

He asked me why we had moved from Kellyville and back to Okmulgee. I just told him it was because that was what Mom wanted. I also let him know that she and Dad were separated and that he now lived in Texas.

Marc was still quiet most of the time, but I was happy walking around the park with him and feeling the warmth of his hand holding mine.

When we left the park, he drove us back to Uncle Doug's, walked me to the front door, and told me to say hi to Mom. He told me he had promised his dad to have the car back by seven, so he couldn't stay any longer.

"Take care of yourself, Lori. I hope we can see each other again soon. I'll write and stay in touch with you when I can," he said and hugged me goodbye.

Nothing exciting ever happened to me when I was with Marc. Nothing ever seemed to go anywhere or change when we were together. Everything always remained the same, even the fast beating of my heart when I was with him. The butterflies still fluttered in my stomach when I looked into his eyes.

I was glad that he now had my new address and phone number, so we could at least write to each other and keep in touch. I knew his mom would not get her hands on this one.

CHAPTER 36

Terrell's Trip to Texas, Early 1953

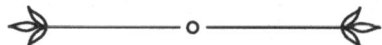

Driving back home to Okmulgee after visiting Mom's brother, Terrell and I found out why Mom was feeling so happy. She told us that she had heard from Dad and that he now has a good job. He wanted us to come to Texas and live with him again as a family.

Mom told us that she had agreed to let Terrell visit with him for a few weeks so she would have more time to think about all of us moving. Mom asked Terrell how he would feel about staying with Dad for a little while. Terrell told Mom he would like to do that.

Mom said if things worked out after Terrell's visit, we would all move to the Texas Gulf Coast. She then asked me what my thoughts were about getting together as a family again.

How could I ever tell her my honest thoughts and my true feelings? How could I tell her that was the one thing I hoped would never happen? How could I say to her that I had secretly hoped and prayed that we would never hear from Dad again?

One of the surprises Dr. Cook had given Mom when he helped move us from Kellyville to Okmulgee was a '49 Plymouth. Mom felt that driving Terrell to Texas in the car he had given her would be safe.

Mom had given Granny her last-minute instructions regarding taking care of Louise and Lee while we were gone, so we were ready to head to Texas. Granny hugged our necks and reminded us that God would be with us on our journey and would take care of us.

I knew that Granny and God were good buddies because she always talked about Him and read His Bible stories to us whenever she had the chance. Granny made sure that Terrell and I were with her every Wednesday evening and Sunday morning when she went to church. She wanted us to learn more about Jesus.

I remembered one particular Sunday morning service when I was sitting next to her listening to the music and the words the preacher was saying seemed to be directed only to me. From his message that morning, I understood that I needed to be closer to the same God that Granny loved so much.

I remember looking at her that Sunday and asking her what I needed to do to be close to God just like she was. I was only twelve at the time, and I didn't understand all of the words she always read to me from her Bible. All I knew was that at that moment, sitting there in church beside her, I wanted to be closer to God. Granny looked down at me, smiled, and told me that all I needed to do was to get baptized and to let God know that I loved and wanted Him in my life.

That following Sunday, I was dressed in a striking white dress Granny had bought me, and I got baptized. So when Granny told us that God would take care of us as we left to go to Texas, I knew she was right.

It was a long drive from Okmulgee to Texas, and we tried to make the best of it. Mom turned on the car radio, and we sang many of the songs that were playing. I remembered the silly games we played when we drove to Tulsa and the funny Burma Shave signs along the highway to read, so playing games again helped pass the time.

On our way, I asked Terrell if he was excited about staying with Dad for a few weeks.

"I guess, Lori. I hope he's not as mean as he used to be," he said.

After the long drive and many pit stops, we made it to Clute, Texas. Mom had no trouble finding where Dad had told her he was living. It was a tiny trailer in a small trailer park at the edge of town.

As soon as we started getting out of the car, Dad saw us. He first hugged Mom and then turned to Terrell and hugged him. He then turned and hugged me. The coldness I felt when he hugged me was something I hadn't felt in a long time. I knew I had to shake it off and be happy for Mom, as she was in tears already just being near her husband again.

The next day, after we had rested from the trip, Dad spent the day just driving us around and showing us everything he could. Of course, the beach was the best place to be. It was fun just watching the seagulls looking for fish to catch. We loved to stand and watch the ocean waves gently come ashore. The current would always bring new shells or sea moss from the ocean to shore. It was fun digging through all of it to see what we could find.

Dad then drove us to the giant chemical company where he worked. He told Mom it paid well, and for once, he was ready to settle down and be the husband and father he knew he could be.

Dad also told her he wanted nothing more than for her and his kids to move to Texas and be with him. Dad promised Mom while we were driving around that he would find the right place for us to move to, and it would be one that would make us all feel proud. Mom told him she would give it some thought after Terrell spent time with him. She wanted to be sure this time that it would be the right move for all of us as a family.

After a few days of staying in that tiny trailer, Mom and I were ready to return to Okmulgee. It felt strange leaving Terrell behind. I hoped with all my heart that Dad would be good to him and care for him as a father should. I know Mom felt the same as I saw the tears running down her cheeks when we said goodbye and drove away, leaving Terrell with Dad.

It was almost 60 years later, during a visit with Terrell, that I found out some things that happened when he spent those few weeks with Dad back in 1953. As adults that day, Terrell and I started talking and reliving our past, sharing things we had never shared before.

Terrell and his wife Sharon lived about 300 miles away, so we didn't see each other more than once or twice a year. The three of us had just finished our lunch and were still sitting at my kitchen table when Terrell and I started talking about our past.

I knew our dad had a way about him that put fear into you about sharing anything that may happen in his presence, so I was not surprised at the things Terrell opened up and shared with me that day. Terrell had suppressed those things and had never shared them with anyone, including Mom. He had been living with secrets, just as I had been all those years—personal secrets that neither of us had ever shared with anyone. The fear Dad put in Terrell had made him bury things that had happened during his stay in Texas. That fear, even after sixty years, was what had kept anyone from finding out just how he had been treated until he opened up and told me.

Terrell told me that one of the first things Dad did was move them to a one-room efficiency located in the front of the trailer park. Terrell said he spent most of his time sleeping on the couch and watching TV. When Dad would come home from work, they would play cards and watch more TV.

He also told me they would go to the beach on the weekends when Dad was not working. Dad would go to one of the bars to drink beer, but he would first give the car keys to Terrell and tell him to drive up and down the beach until he saw him coming out and ready to leave. Then Dad would take the keys and drive them back to the trailer park. Terrell reminded me that he was only twelve years old then but was big for his age, so he was never stopped or questioned by the patrol cars that drove past him.

We both remembered during our talk that Dad always demanded full respect; "Yes sir" or "No sir" was required. He would tell us to refer to him as Mr. Bevins if we were around strangers. We remembered that we would get into trouble about anything we would say or do that Dad didn't like. So Terrell said he did what Dad told him to do and drove up and down the beach until he saw Dad walk out of the beer joint.

Terrell also shared with me one of the punishments he remembered. He told me that one time Dad drove them to a country road nearby, stopped next to a wooded area, and told him to get a switch off of one of the trees so he could spank him. Dad told him not to come back with a small one because if he did, he would get a bigger one!

Terrell told me that Dad would lean him against the back of the car and spank him with the switch. He recalled that tears never came to his eyes, no matter how much it hurt. Terrell said he would repeatedly tell himself that he would soon be back home with Mom, so he knew he could endure anything Dad wanted to do to him.

The conversation that Terrell and I had those sixty years later in our lives made me quite sure that more had to have taken place during his stay with Dad in Texas. But the pain, punishment, and fear that Dad had put in him made him bury things deep inside, and there was nothing else he wanted to share.

CHAPTER 37

Mom Makes a Decision, 1953

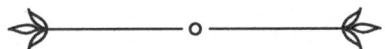

The drive back home from Texas with Mom after leaving Terrell with Dad was quiet. She didn't talk much, and I knew her mind was going in different directions. She knew she just had to wait and see how Terrell's stay with Dad in Texas would be. That would help her decide what she needed to do.

I didn't have much to say either. All I could think about was maybe having to leave Okmulgee and move again. I was happy there and couldn't think about moving to Texas. I would miss school, my friends, and my granny. What would I do if Mom decided that we should move again?

Those few weeks of summer, while Mom was making up her mind, are my favorite times to look back on. My cousin Ellen and I spent most of our time just sitting in one of the apple trees at Grandpa Howard's orchard, eating green apples and having fun. We also went on long walks along the railroad tracks and acted silly.

When we got the chance, we would go to the root beer stand near our high school and just sit and visit our school buddies. That was the favorite hangout for all our friends during the summer.

It was there that I met Gene. It didn't take long for the two of us to get acquainted. I liked his sense of humor, and he said my smile was cute. One afternoon he asked me out for a date. I missed dating Gary, and I felt that Marc was someone I just needed to forget, so I agreed to go out with him.

Our first date was fun. Gene drove us out to the lake, and we just spent time talking. Gene was easy to talk to, and he made me laugh. I found myself just relaxing and enjoying being with him.

Gene was a couple of years older than me, but we enjoyed each other. On our first date, he asked me if I attended a church in town, and I told him yes. I told him I always went to church with my granny. He wanted to know where it was and what time we were going.

That following Sunday, he was there with Granny and me, sitting in the pew, holding his Bible in his hands, and reading it along with the preacher. I knew then that he was going to be very different. Granny and Mom liked him; he became a part of our family almost overnight.

Summer was coming to an end, and I knew the time was coming when Mom would need to decide if she would move us to Texas. I was hoping that her decision would be *no*. I didn't want any part of moving to Texas!

I decided to ask Mom if she would allow me to stay in Okmulgee and live with my aunt and uncle if she decided to return to Dad. Ellen and I had already talked to my aunt and uncle to see if they would let me live with them, and they said yes. I loved the school I was attending, my cousin Ellen, and my granny with all my heart, and I had come to care very much for Gene. Moving away was not what I wanted at all.

And I wanted no part of Dad again! I had buried our past as deep as I could. But the fear of being around him again was still there.

We had moved so many times, even before we moved to Pryor when the judge had put Dad in jail. My life had to change every time we moved. I had given up schools, friendships, and Marc more often than I wanted to remember. Our last big move was from Kellyville to Okmulgee when Mom discovered that Dad was back in the bootlegging business with Roger Clements and sent him away. I was tired of making new friends repeatedly and never being able to stay in touch with any of them, Marc especially.

Marc was always special to me. No matter who I met or what boy I dated, Marc was always tucked someplace deep in my heart. We always tried to make sure that we had each other's phone numbers and addresses to keep in touch. I feared that if Mom moved our family to Texas, I would never see him again.

The following Sunday after church, Gene left to return to his dorm at college, and Mom asked me if I would go to the store with her. I thought it strange, as she had never asked me to do that before.

It wasn't a trip to the store Mom took us to but a drive to the park. Mom stopped the car and told me she needed to talk to me. I knew then what she had on her mind.

"Lori, I have talked to Terrell and your dad, and I've decided I'm taking you and the twins to Texas to bring our family together again," she told me.

I had to tell her! I had to tell Mom I didn't want to go with her to Texas. I wanted to stay in Okmulgee and live with Uncle Chuck and Aunt Sue.

Mom looked at me and said, "Lori, I know you are happy here, but you'll be okay when we move to Texas! You will make new friends and adjust to a new school, and it will be the last time we will have to move."

"It's not that, Mom. I don't want to move to Texas because I don't want to be around Dad," I told her.

"Lori, what in the world makes you say a thing like that? I know he is strict and makes all of you behave, but he is your dad, and you need to respect that," she said.

With tears beginning to form in my eyes, I looked at Mom and told her, "Mom, Dad has done things to me that you do not know. He made me promise him long ago when we lived in Tulsa that I would never tell you about what he did to me. He told me that you would never love me again if I told you. He let me know what he was doing to me and what he was teaching me to do was to make me a better woman when I grew up. He felt he needed to be the one to teach me about sex, so he would do things to me and have me do things with him so I could learn. I was always afraid to be around him. He had me afraid to ever tell anyone. But I'm telling you now, Mom. I know those things were all bad, and I never want to be near him again!"

Mom became furious and unhappy with me as soon as I told her those things about Dad. Her voice was shaky as she said to me, "I don't believe a word you just said. How could you come up with something like that? Are you saying this hoping I'll let you stay in Okmulgee? I'm so upset with you, Lori, for even thinking these things. You need to think hard about what you've just told me and then forget we had this talk. You're going with me to Texas, and I never want to hear about this conversation again."

Mom then drove us home without saying another word and told me to go in and tell Granny she would be back home soon. Later that night, Gene walked in the door with Mom and helped her to her bedroom.

After he helped her get into her bed, he closed the door, then told us what had happened. "The police stopped her because she ran a red light, and after they talked to her for a short time, they took her to jail because she had been drinking and was not in any condition to continue driving. After she sobered up, one of the officers let her call someone to take her home, and she called me," he told us.

Gene also told us that she didn't want to talk to any of us. She just wanted him to get her home and to her bedroom, leave her alone, and close the door.

It was late the next afternoon when Mom came out of her bedroom. She let us all know that she was okay and that we all needed to help her start packing as we were all moving to Texas.

CHAPTER 38

The Move to Texas, 1953

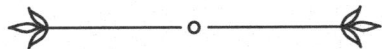

The new home Dad said he would have ready for all of us to move to was a total joke! Had all the lies he had made to her in the past made Mom think he would stop lying? The new home he moved us to was in the middle of a row of five army barracks. Our new home consisted of two large rooms and was right next to the main highway that led into Freeport, Texas.

Mom and Dad had a bedroom to sleep in with a tiny bathroom tucked in the corner. The other room was the kitchen area. That's where the four of us would sleep. That was our bedroom and the kitchen. Dad had bought four cots and placed them in the middle of the room for us to use as our beds.

The barracks were not only near the main highway; they were also close to a noisy bowling alley, and just outside one of the windows in our kitchen bedroom was a skating rink that was under a tent.

We had no telephone and just two lights on the ceiling. I asked Mom where we were supposed to eat and put our clothes.

Mom put her arm around my shoulders and told me we would go shopping and find a table, chairs, and a couple of dressers. Dad stood there trying to explain that this was only a temporary place for us to live. He said that the chemical company he had gone to work for was new and growing fast, and it was building housing as quickly as possible. Dad said we needed to be patient, and he would make sure that we moved to a better place soon.

Again, he had Mom in his clutches and knew she would understand and make the most of the situation. Mom always found a way to make things better. Her willpower and her love for Dad always found a way.

I couldn't wait to get outside and walk around to see what and who lived close to us. I could see we would have close neighbors. I just hoped they would be good ones.

I soon noticed a group gathered in a circle around a big pot sitting on a fire they had made. The people around it were a mixture of children and adults. My curiosity got the best of me, so I had to join them.

I looked down in the big pot to see what they were all fussing over, and all I could see was a bunch of funny-looking things with claws moving around in the water.

I asked the young man standing nearby what was in there, and he just laughed and said, "You must be new to the Gulf Coast!"

"Yes, I'm from Oklahoma, and we just moved here, so what's that?" I asked him.

He introduced himself as Clifford and said, "This is what we do here to stay entertained and have some fun, and besides that, they're fun to eat."

EAT! How terrible, I thought. Those things looked nasty!

"What are they?" I asked Clifford.

"They are called crabs, and you catch them at the jetties near here and then cook them in what is known as a crab boil. Then you crack open the shell and eat the meat inside. It is delicious," he told me.

About that time, Mom and Dad, the twins, and Terrell walked to where we were standing, and Dad explained all of this to Mom and told her that he would take us all to the jetties tomorrow and show us how to catch them.

Terrell told me that he had learned to do this while staying with Dad, and it was fun, so that was good to know. At least there would be something to do besides stay inside that army barrick that was supposed to be our new home.

We spent the next few days shopping for a table and chairs and a dresser to have a place to put our clothes. We also went crabbing together, which was fun, and I discovered real fast that they could hurt you with those claws if you were not careful.

At the next crab boil a few days later, Clifford showed me how to shell the crabs and eat the meat. I knew it wasn't wrong to cook and eat them; it was just the idea that we were eating something so ugly to look at that I didn't like.

Trying to sleep at night was hard. I moved my cot as close as possible to the window, placed my head on my pillow, and watched the people roller skate as I listened to the loud music.

I had never skated, but I watched and knew I could learn. That next day I found Clifford, and I asked him if he knew how to skate. He said he did.

Then he asked me if I knew how, and I told him no. But I wanted to learn. It didn't take him long to let me know he would like to teach me, and he asked if I would like to go skating that evening. Of course I said yes, but first I asked him what the cost would be, and he told me since I would be going with him, he would take care of the cost.

Skating was so much fun, and Clifford was too. I found out he went to the same school I would be attending. He told me that since he had a car, I could ride with him, and I wouldn't have to ride the bus. I told him I would have to check with my mom to make sure it would be okay.

Mom said that would be great, as she would have to take Terrell and the twins to different schools about seven miles away. This would save her some time, and she wouldn't have to worry about how I was getting to school.

We had to start our new schools at the end of the school year. The move we had made from Oklahoma to Texas and going to a new school was hard on us.

I was getting tired of having to do this over and over again. Not knowing anyone made me feel lost, mad, and unhappy. I wanted to feel loved.

The new school I attended was not what I had hoped it would be. I didn't like any of the subjects or the teachers. I would find an empty table when it was lunchtime, and when I finished eating, I would go to the girls' bathroom and sit on the floor until it was time to return to class. I had no desire to meet new friends.

Clifford tried introducing me to some of his friends, but I didn't want to get close to anyone. It hurt too much to make friends and then lose them. So I decided to stay to myself and do my best to get through each day. I was also doing everything I could to stay away from Dad and not be angry with Mom since she had chosen not to believe me and made me move to Texas with her.

Mom soon found that she could load all of us up and head to the beach on weekends or when we got home from school and Dad was at work to keep us entertained. We would spend the entire time just playing in the sand and picking up shells. We learned that we could dig a deep hole in the sand, place some wood in the hole, and then cook. We would wrap whatever we were cooking in foil and then let it cook while we played in the ocean.

After a few months of living in that tiny two-room army barrack, Mom found us a place to move. She loved exploring roads and new neighborhoods. One day as we were driving around, she saw a "for rent" sign on a house and stopped to ask about it.

Mom was excited when she returned to the car after talking to the people that owned the home and told us that we would be moving there soon. We were all very excited, as my brothers and sister didn't care about our current living area either.

Mom didn't take long to get Dad to agree and make arrangements for our move. New furniture and beds, not cots, were the first thing that Mom got. She also found a couch, a few chairs, and a table where we could sit and eat. Life was starting to get better!

Moving to that house meant so much to all of us. The house was on a large lot and had three bedrooms. So Terrell and I had a room, the twins had their room, and Mom and Dad had a room. Our kitchen had all the things we needed, and we were delighted.

It was quite a distance from the school I was attending, so I had to ride a school bus instead of going with Clifford, but that was okay with me.

I often wondered if Mom had said anything to Dad about the conversation she and I had before moving to Texas. It was evident that he paid very little attention to me and never once reached out to hug or get close when we were near each other. He avoided me most of the time, and I was grateful for that. But it did cross my mind several times why he treated me so differently. Not at all like his special princess. So I truly believed that Mom had said something to him.

The school year was coming to an end in a few weeks. It had been tough starting a new school in the middle of the last semester, so I was grateful it was ending. I had not allowed anyone to get close to me as a friend. My life was me doing what I could do to face each day as it came.

I wanted more than anything to have Granny, Ellen, or Gene there, but most of all, I wanted to be able to see and talk to Marc. It had been almost a year since Marc and I talked to each other. Marc told me then that he would make sure he got any letter I would send him and would write back, but I had already sent several to him and had not received an answer. I knew I needed to get over him, so I buried him deep in my heart, where he would have to stay.

CHAPTER 39

A Visit from Gene: Clute, Texas, 1954

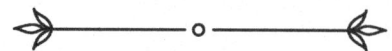

Our school was out for the summer, and I was outside enjoying the sun when Mom told me someone wanted me on the phone. She had a funny grin as she called me inside and handed me the phone. The voice on the other end of the phone sounded strange to me.

"Hi, Lori. This is Gene. How are you?" he said.

"Gene, is this you? I'm so surprised. How in the world did you get my number?" I asked him.

"Your mom told me she would call and give it to me when your family found a home and settled somewhere. I hope this doesn't make you mad at her or me!" he said.

"Oh, Gene, I'm not mad at all. I'm thrilled to hear your voice. How are you?" I asked.

"I'm fine, Lori. I would love to come and visit with you for at least a week if that is okay. I've already got permission from your mom. I need to know if that is something that you'll agree to."

"Gene, I would love to see you and have you here to visit for a week. When can you come?" I asked him.

"Not soon enough since I know you want to see me. I joined the Navy Reserve after graduating from college and have a leave starting next week. I can be there in about ten days, and I can't wait to see you!" he said.

That was the longest ten days I had ever spent. I was so excited to know I would be with someone I cared for and who also cared for me. I always felt so safe being with Gene. He had never crossed the line with me, but I always knew he wanted to.

I told Mom that I was grateful to her for staying in touch with him and letting him know where we would be. I knew she had a close bond with him, but I didn't realize how close it was. She told me she wanted to see me smile again and look happy, and she knew Gene could make that happen.

A few days later, without my knowledge, Gene called Mom when his bus got in town, and she left to go pick him up. I noticed Mom when she left but had no idea where she was going.

I was outside when Mom returned and pulled up in the driveway. I then saw Gene step out of the passenger side. What a wonderful happy moment that was. Gene was almost in tears as he grabbed me and gave me a wonderful bear hug.

At that moment, life was good again, and I was thrilled to see him. I hugged him back as tight as possible, wanting that moment to last forever.

The week that I spent with Gene was full of mixed emotions! One moment I thought I loved him dearly, and the next moment I felt he was nothing but a very dear friend. We had a fun week that was crammed full of things we did, and in the evenings, we would throw a blanket on the grass outside to sit and talk.

On the last day that Gene was going to be there, he asked Dad if he could borrow the car so he could take me for a ride. I had no idea what Gene had in mind other than just wanting us to be alone.

After driving around, Gene found a place to pull up and stop that was not around anyone or anything. He reached over, pulled me close to him, and told me that he was in love with me and wanted me to think about us getting married when he got out of the Navy and I got out of school.

I was surprised! I knew Gene greatly cared for me, but I was still unsure how I truly felt about him. Before I could answer him, he started going too far with the hugging and the kissing—much further than I wanted him to.

"Gene, stop! I want you to know that I care for you very much, but I'm not ready for this! Please let me have time to think about it, and I'll let you know," I told him.

After a few moments of silence, Gene pulled away. "I'm sorry, Lori. I care so much for you and want you to know that I'm serious about us getting married," he told me.

"I know, Gene, and I want you to understand I've had a wonderful time with you. I'm so glad you came when you did. I've been so lonely and wanted to see someone I knew cared for me. I'm not too fond of this place in Texas, and I want to be back in Oklahoma more than anything. So let me have time to consider us getting married." I went on, explaining, "I've never understood why Mom moved us here in the first place! I was happy in Okmulgee being with my friends and Granny and Ellen and you. I hated it so much when she decided we would move here, and I begged her to let me stay there and live with my aunt and uncle. I have resented her since we moved here. I told her I didn't want to be around my dad. I'm not happy here at all."

"Lori, don't you know why your mom decided to move you all to Texas?" he asked.

"No, Gene, I have no idea. I only know how much she loves Dad and wants to be with him now since he has a good job."

He looked puzzled, and I felt he was thinking about what he would say. "Do you remember the night your mom had too much to drink, and I was the one she called to get her out of jail?" he asked.

"Oh, I remember that night very well," I replied.

"Lori, your mom told me that night when I picked her up from the police station what you said to her that evening. How you told her about how your dad had abused you when you were younger. But she didn't believe you. She thought you were making it up so you wouldn't have to move to Texas. Of course it upset her, so she started drinking and didn't stop. Dr. Cook had also told her that she no longer had a job or a home for all of you. It was just too much! She told me that she knew she had to move all of you to Texas, but it was not what she wanted to do. It was because she had no choice.

"Dr. Cook had told your mom that same day that his wife had found out just how close the two of them were, and she made him promise to fire your mom and move her out of the house he was providing for all of you or she would divorce him.

"Your mom knew that she could not support all of you without a job. She had to take your dad up on his offer to care for all of you. And that meant she would have to move to Texas. Your mom confided in me and asked me to promise I would never say anything to you about it. That is one of the reasons we have such a strong friendship," he explained.

Granny had always told me that there is always a reason for everything in life, so now I knew why Gene was there by my side at that very moment. Suddenly, life lifted the disappointment and the hurt I had been keeping for my mom all that time. I suddenly understood everything and realized my mom did what she had to do to take care of my brothers, sister, and me.

"Gene, I'm so glad you let me know all this. It makes so much sense now. I'm also sad that you know about my dad. I wasn't lying to Mom about that at all. He hasn't tried anything with me since we moved here, so hopefully, he has changed. But I'll still always make sure that I'm never alone with him because I'll never trust him again."

Gene hugged and kissed me and told me one more time that he loved me and hoped I would write to him as soon as he got back to Oklahoma, and that I would say yes to his proposal of marriage.

Mom and I drove him to the bus station the following day, and as I waved goodbye, I felt this would be the last time I would see him. I knew what he meant to me. It was a good feeling, but not deep enough for me to marry him.

I gave my mom a big hug that evening and told her that I loved her and was so grateful for her contacting Gene so we could see each other. I told her it had made me happy, and I thanked her for being such a wonderful mother.

From the smile I saw on her face, I genuinely believe that she felt things would be different between us now. The grudge and disappointment I had been holding against her were gone, and I hoped she could see it in my face.

CHAPTER 40

Meeting Robert

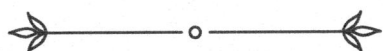

The summer was almost over, and I was glad I'd had that short visit with Gene. The school year would soon begin, and I wasn't looking forward to the coming year. I was going to be in the eleventh grade and knew I could make it for two more years if I worked at it.

Fishing, crabbing, and going to the beach filled the summer with some pleasure, so I decided that Texas was not that bad. I had to convince myself that when eleventh grade started, I would need to have a new attitude about making friends and having fun.

After the visit from Gene during the summer, I knew I had to write him and let him know how I felt. In my letter, I had to tell him that I cared for him as a friend but had no intentions of marriage or even having him as a boyfriend. I had to make sure that he knew he was very special to me, but it couldn't go any further. After several weeks passed and I didn't get a letter back from him, I assumed he was okay with what I had told him in my letter.

At the end of the summer, Dad got a big promotion at the plant where he worked, and Mom decided that she would return to work as a nurse as soon as the twins were in school. Life was getting better for us as a family, and I knew I needed to change my way of thinking to improve my life.

Since Mom and Dad both had good jobs, Mom convinced Dad that we needed to own our own home, not rent one. Finding one she liked in a nearby town didn't take long. It was also in an area where we wouldn't have to change schools. It would mean another move for us, but this time to a wonderful home of our own and a beautiful neighborhood.

Our new home was in a town where a school bus would pick all of us up close to our house and take us to school. That pleased Mom, as she could go to work and not worry about getting us to school.

Another wonderful thing Mom did when we got ready to move was arrange to have Granny come from Okmulgee so she could live with us again. That way, Granny would be there for all of us when we got home from school since she had decided to go back to work.

It was a fantastic day for me when Mom and I went to the bus station to pick her up. Granny was a big part of my life again, so I knew I could handle anything. The world took on a new beginning with Granny with us once again.

As soon as school started, I discovered nothing in the eleventh grade would be easy.

Teachers taught differently in every school I had attended. Math was the hardest, and then learning Texas history was a joke. I didn't care about Texas history because I was from Oklahoma! Physical education and our swimming class were evil! I had never been a swimmer and didn't even enjoy being in the water. My PE teacher in my swimming class decided that I would swim or drown. Well, I almost did, *twice*. So, of course I made terrible grades in her class. I didn't do well in Texas history or math class either. I think home economics was my best class, and maybe English.

The only fun I had going to school was that I had started making new friends. I made two nice girlfriends and was not doing too bad in making friends with the boys. To me, it was easier to bond with boys instead of girls.

I didn't go for all the primping and silliness most girls did. To me, a lot of them were just fake. Boys were themselves and didn't pretend to be anything else.

One of my new friends, Wanda, became a special friend to me. We were on the same level in many ways. She often invited me to visit her home on weekends to spend time with her. I also grew to care very much for both her mom and dad. They would drive over and pick me up from my house on the weekends so we could spend time together.

Then one unforgettable weekend, Wanda's brother Robert came home on leave. He had graduated from our school a year before and joined the Navy.

Robert was older than me, and I liked him right away. I think the feeling was mutual, as he asked me for a date within the first two days of his being home. Of course I said yes, because I was eager to start dating again, and he was so cute!

Wanda was excited about me dating her brother. She told me he didn't have a girlfriend and knew he needed one. Of course, at that time in my life, I was seeking the attention I had missed from not having a boyfriend or someone to date.

Our first date was fun, and I soon realized that Robert was just a happy-go-lucky person. Nothing seemed to bother him. On our second date, we drove out to where his father worked. It was a small building in the middle of a large open field. I didn't know what his dad did for a living, but Robert told me he was an inspector checking this location out for his company.

While there, Robert spotted a yellow cactus plant out in the middle of the field that had a beautiful bloom. He asked me if I thought it was pretty, and of course I said yes, as it was beautiful.

Then he walked out into the open field, returned with the bloom, and handed it to me.

"Lori, you can have this if you promise me you will go to dinner with me tonight," he said, smiling.

His dad looked at me and grinned. "Be sure the thorns are all off before he hands it to you, as you may get stuck! And be careful tonight, as you never know what this boy will come up with next," he said.

I left that field feeling happy and content. I knew that the kindness and warmth of these new people in my life were what I needed. My mind could not help but wonder where it may be taking me.

I soon found out that Robert was very much a romantic person. He made each date he took me on special for the next two weeks. He would always meet me at the door with one flower in his hand to give to me. Robert never tried to take advantage of me and was always a perfect gentleman. He made me feel special, and I loved the feeling he gave me inside.

One of his favorite things to do was wait outside my classroom door so that he could walk me to my next class. I noticed a few heads would turn when he did. He never missed a day doing that when he was home on leave, and having a good-looking guy in a white sailor's uniform walk me through the halls was fun. Come to think of it, Mom was a nurse dressed in white all the time. Maybe that was one of my attractions to Robert.

Driving me home from school was at the top of his to-do list, so I didn't have to ride the bus. But for some reason, he would never come into my house. He would drop me off and tell me he would call me later.

Two weeks was all he had left before he had to go overseas. Robert told me he would be gone for a few months but would love for me to write to him and help pass the time until he could return. He told me he had come to care for me very much. He asked me to keep a place in my heart for him until he returned home.

My goodbye hug and kiss with him when he had to leave was hard to handle. He had brought so much peace into my life for such a short time, but

I knew I was blessed to have had it while I did. Now I needed to return to studying for my upcoming twelfth grade and graduation from school.

My evenings at home felt safe since Granny was always there. I wasn't afraid of my dad anymore, but I was wise enough never to take a chance of being around him alone. Would I ever forget or forgive him for the past? In my heart, I wanted to, and I wanted to feel safe around him.

I loved having Granny around. She would sit and talk to me if the twins were busy elsewhere when she had the chance. She did ask me one evening about my new boyfriend, Robert. "What is it that you see in him?" she asked me.

"Granny, he's easy to be around, for one thing, and he's always a perfect gentleman with me, never trying anything that most boys do," I told her.

"That does speak a lot for him. Does he go to church?" she asked.

"I think so, Granny, but we have never talked about it," I told her.

Then she asked me if I still sent letters to Marc and if I knew how he was doing. That threw me for a loop, as I hadn't thought of him for quite some time.

"No, Granny, I haven't because he quit answering the letters I sent him, so I had to assume that he no longer cared," I told her.

"Well, Lori, if I were you, I would try again because you never know. Didn't you tell me once that his mom would always get the letters before he did and throw them away?" she asked.

"Yes, but he said he would watch for the mail and try and get to it first," I said.

That night as I lay there in bed, my mind would not shut down! Maybe Granny was right. Perhaps I should try again to find out how Marc was and if he still cared about me.

As I fell asleep, my mind was composing the letter, and I tried to make sure I would be saying the right things to him when I wrote it. Should I tell him about Robert? Should I tell Marc he has always been the one I wanted, no matter who I had dated for the past few years?

I received many letters from Robert, and I did write back to him, but not as often as he had hoped. For some reason, my heart was just not there. He kept asking me why I didn't write more often, and I would tell him that I was working hard trying to make it to the twelfth grade and didn't have the time. I struggled with school, and my grades were acceptable, but I knew I would make it to the twelfth grade if I tried hard enough.

I decided to go ahead and write a letter to Marc. I had to rewrite it several times to make sure it sounded right, and then I mailed it. I hoped I would hear back from him but wondered if he would even get it before his mom did.

CHAPTER 41

A Surprise from Dad, 1954

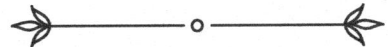

A surprise gift that Dad gave me made my life more fun during the last few months of school. Dad loved gambling and playing poker games with the men at work. Gambling was how he survived the year that Mom kicked him out. He had spent almost a year just going from town to town drinking and gambling, with nothing on his mind other than fun, so he was good at playing the games.

He won a car during his poker game with his current gambling buddies and gave it to me as a special early birthday gift. The only rule he told me when he gave it to me was that I had to pay for the gas, and if I ever got a ticket for any reason, he would take the car away from me.

This new early birthday gift was a beautiful yellow Chrysler convertible with wooden side paneling. It was very different from any car you would usually see in our little town and stood out among all the other vehicles driving around. I loved it and knew I'd take excellent care of it. I already had my driver's license, so that wouldn't be a problem, but paying for gas would be.

A Dairy Queen was close to us, and I would go there after school a lot because that was where my school bus let me off. I often stopped there to get some ice cream, and I remembered seeing a "help wanted" sign in the window a few days earlier.

It didn't take me long to go there and apply for the job, and I got it! My hours would be from 4 p.m. until 10 p.m. Monday through Friday, and from

10 a.m. to 5 p.m. on Saturday and Sunday. My new boss was kind, and the crew I would work with were all my age or a little older.

The pay was fifty cents an hour, which would help pay for my gas. I was glad I could now drive to school and back home in my car and not have to ride the school bus.

I was a hit at school when I started showing up in that beautiful yellow convertible, and before I knew it, some of my friends were asking me if I would pick them up so they would not have to ride the school bus.

Of course I agreed with a couple of friends, but only if they were willing to help me pay for gas. I charged them twenty-five cents each time I drove them to school. I loved all the attention my new convertible gave me. And I didn't have to spend my own money driving around.

A few weeks had passed since I had mailed my letter off to Marc, and I was stunned when I got a letter back from him so quickly. It was short and direct, but it was at least a letter. Marc was a year ahead of me in school, and he wanted me to know that he planned on joining the Air National Guard as soon as he graduated. He told me he would be at Lackland Air Force Base in San Antonio, Texas, and, if possible, he would like to see me during that time. He signed his letter "Love, Marc."

I had been waiting almost two years to hear from him, and now that I had, I was more confused about my future and life than ever. Did I dare still hang on to hopes of him? Could I count on seeing him and moving forward after all that time? Did I read things into the word "Love" he had used to sign his letter? I felt so confused. I wasn't sure that what Robert and I had was love. I wasn't sure of a lot of things.

CHAPTER 42

My Senior Prom, 1954

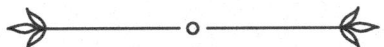

Time passed by very fast, and before I knew it, Robert was back home. I was happy he was back. It didn't take long for him to call me and take me out on a date, and I had forgotten how much fun he was and how nicely he treated me.

It felt great having someone treat me special. Robert had a way of doing that. We could talk to each other about anything and find fun in everything we did.

The Junior-Senior Prom was coming up at school, so I asked him if he would be my date. Of course he said yes. A naval base was nearby, and Robert was free most evenings and weekends. That made it easy for us to spend a lot of time together, and Robert quickly became a significant part of my life again.

Mom and I went shopping the following week for a dress I could wear to the prom. I found one that I liked that made me feel pretty. Mom told me it made me look very grown-up when I tried it on.

When Robert picked me up the night of the prom, I told him he looked handsome in his white suit and bow tie, and he told me he thought I looked beautiful in my dress. We were both ready to dance the night away, which is what we did, and it was so much fun!

We left before the prom was over because Robert told me he wanted to drive to the beach. When we got to his car, he pulled out a bottle of wine from the back seat. Before we even left the parking lot, he told me that we needed to have a special drink to celebrate the evening.

I had never had wine before but soon realized I liked it. To me, it tasted just like grape juice. I had a few more drinks of wine on our drive to the beach, and by the time we got there, I was beginning to feel a little silly. Robert laughed at me and said that maybe I shouldn't drink anymore!

"Why?" I asked. "It's delicious, and I'm thirsty."

The beach Robert wanted to drive to was not our local beach. He wanted to go to the beach in Galveston, a forty-five-minute drive from where we were. When we got there, Robert parked the car and said, "Let's go for a walk Lori. I need to talk to you, and the night is beautiful."

The moon was beautiful, and the sound of the water from the ocean was calm and peaceful. Robert was holding my hand when he suddenly stopped and turned to face me.

"Lori, our relationship has been short, and we haven't been together that much, but I want you to know you are the one I want to be with now and for the rest of my life. Will you accept me as your sweetheart and your husband one day with this ring I want to place on your finger?" he asked.

I wasn't prepared for that at all! It took me as a complete surprise. Being his wife had never crossed my mind. However, he made me feel happy and safe, so why shouldn't I accept the ring and see what happens in the future?

"Yes, Robert, I'll accept your ring and promise to be your sweetheart. Just give me time to get out of school and see what the future brings me," I answered.

"That's all I can ask of you, Lori. I want you to finish school and make sure that you want to be with me, as bad as I want to be with you," he replied.

When we returned to the car, I felt like I needed another drink of wine. I should have left the wine alone like Robert had told me because halfway home, I started getting sick and had to get him to pull the car over so I could throw up! It was no longer any fun to drink wine. All I wanted was to get home and go to bed.

Robert drove me home walked me to my door and gave me a sweet kiss goodnight. He told me he loved me and to get a good night's sleep, and he would talk to me tomorrow

Little did we know what awaited us when we reached my front door. Dad was standing there watching us and yelled at Robert as he walked away, saying he was not happy with him getting me home at two a.m.! He yelled at him as he was leaving and told him to stop dating me if he couldn't get me home at a decent time!

I felt so bad for Robert. Why did Dad have to do that?

"Dad, you should have left him alone! We had a special night tonight, and you had no right yelling at him!" I told him as we entered the front room.

"What do you mean you had a special night? What made it so special that you didn't remember you were to be home by midnight?" Dad asked me.

"It was special because tonight we got engaged, and he gave me this beautiful ring," I told him.

"He did what?" Dad said.

Dad then pushed me down in a chair in the front room and reached to pull the ring off my finger. I clutched my fist so tight that he couldn't get it off. Then Dad put his knee in the middle of my chest to hold me down and tried again to force it off my finger. There was a strength in my hand that I had no idea existed because no matter how hard he tried, my fist would not open.

I saw over Dad's shoulder that Granny was coming up behind him, and before I knew what happened, she hit him over the head with a cast-iron skillet and told him to get off of me! He went to his knees on the floor, and when he did, I got up and ran to my bedroom. My sweet granny had come to my rescue!

Mom was working the night shift at the hospital that night, so she didn't know what had happened until the next day when Granny told her. After Mom found out about Dad holding me down in the chair with his knee in my chest, she told him he better never again use that type of force on me or any of their children.

I decided not to tell Robert anything about what had happened. I knew he didn't care for Dad from the very start of our relationship. What took place that night was just another reminder: I needed to stay as far away from Dad as possible.

A few weeks later, as I remembered the evening of the prom and all the wine I drank, I realized I wasn't in any condition to think straight at that time. I should not have accepted the ring from Robert. I cared for him, and he treated me with kindness, but being engaged and letting him think I might marry him was not right.

I also thought deeply about why I cared for or didn't care for most of the boys I had dated. I would always break the relationship up if they tried to get aggressive with me after a few dates.

I also realized that if any of them in the past just wanted to stay as friends and only wanted a kiss now and then, I would stay with them longer. When I let things happen with Gary back in Okmulgee, I knew it was because it was something I wanted and not forced on me. I also knew Gary would leave soon to go off to college and would no longer be part of my life.

Robert was kind and gentle and never stepped over the line or got fresh with me, so I know that's why I stayed with him. Being afraid of sex and being forced into doing things that I didn't like just never worked with me, and I know it had a lot to do with my past.

I also realized that was one of the main reasons I felt the way I did about Marc. He never went beyond holding my hand or placing his arm around my shoulders.

I knew that I needed to break my engagement with Robert. It wasn't fair to him. He cared a lot for me, and I respected that, but love was not a part of it. I just needed to get the courage to let him know, but how?

My school was almost over, and the summer months were just around the corner. I was glad my job at the Dairy Queen took up much of my time. I started saving my money the best I could and took one day at a time, unsure what my next step would be. I needed to give Robert back his ring, but at the same time, I kept thinking maybe I should agree to marry him.

CHAPTER 43

A Surprise Phone Call, 1954

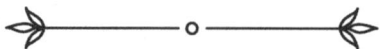

Once again, on August 26, 1954, my life took a turn! I had a phone call from Marc.

When I answered the phone, the voice said "Hi," and I knew who it was at once. Marc had called to remind me that he joined the Air National Guard when he graduated and was at Lackland Air Force Base in San Antonio, Texas. He knew it was not too far from where we lived in Lake Jackson.

Marc told me he had received a telephone call from my mom just before he left for Lackland, and she thought it would be a good idea for us to see each other while he was in Texas.

I don't remember to this day what I said back to him or what else we said in that short conversation, but I do remember that my heart didn't slow down to an average beat for almost thirty minutes after hanging up. I had to talk to Mom and find out what they had said to each other.

Mom was at work when I got his phone call, but Granny was there with me, and she knew what was going on in my life. She told me she knew about the phone call Mom had made to Marc. Granny said that she and Mom felt I was making a mistake by planning to marry Robert because they both knew the only one I had ever truly loved was Marc.

Granny told me she and Mom had discussed my plans to marry Robert. They thought it would be best for Marc and me to see each other before that happened. That's when Mom decided to go ahead and call him. She wanted to find out if he would see me and talk to me before I made what they both felt was a mistake.

Granny and Mom agreed that Marc should also know that I had accepted an engagement ring from someone, which they both felt was just not the move I needed to make.

Later that evening, Mom returned home from work and learned that Marc had called me. Mom told me that when she talked to him, he told her he was glad she had called. He told her he wanted to see me and find out if there were still any feelings between us. He also told her that he had never forgotten me. He explained that he didn't even know where we lived and wondered why he hadn't received any letters from me.

He said it had been almost two years since he had heard from me, so he just figured I had forgotten him. Then he asked if there would be any way she could bring me to Lackland so that the two of us could see each other. She told him, "Of course! That's why I called you in the first place."

After Mom explained all this to me, I couldn't stop the flow of emotions I was feeling. After two years of not hearing from Marc, I had tried so hard to bury my thoughts of him. But just knowing that he wanted to see me was all I needed to hear.

Granny hugged me and told me that she was excited for me as she knew I had always kept Marc in my heart, and she had told me many times that maybe tomorrow everything would be okay!

All I needed to do was to wait until Mom could let me know when we would go to Lackland so I could see him.

The next day, after realizing that I was going to see Marc, I took Robert's ring off my finger and put it on a chain around my neck. I would have to wait and see how things went with Marc to know what I needed to do about Robert.

At that time, Robert had been gone for a few months serving his duty in the Navy Reserve, so I didn't need to write and tell him what was happening. He didn't know anything about my relationship with Marc. I had never discussed it with him. I had buried Marc deep in my heart during that time because I felt he no longer cared.

Two weeks later, when I got off work at the Dairy Queen, Mom told me I needed to ask my boss if I could have the next weekend off. She and Wayne, one of Dad's friends, said they wanted to take a short trip and thought it would be good for me to go with them. Mom told me she felt like I needed to take some time off to relax.

I liked the idea of being off work for a few days, so why not just get in the car and go wherever Mom, Dad, and his friend were going? Little did I know what they had in store for me.

The drive that we were on seemed to last for hours. I was lost in my thoughts and paying no attention to where we were or where we were going. It didn't matter to me anyway. All I could think of was when I might get to see Marc and what I would say to him when we did meet.

After a few stops for gas along the way, Dad pulled into a parking area near a building, stopped the car, and got out, saying he would be back in a moment. I wondered where we were and where Dad was going.

"Mom, what's Dad doing?" I asked her.

"Lori, I think you'll see in a little bit where you are and what's going on," she told me.

As I sat there staring out the window from the back seat, I watched a man about 200 yards away walking in our direction. As he got closer, I could see he was holding something in his hand, and he seemed to be reading whatever it was.

Since he was looking down, I couldn't see his face, but I noticed that he was in a military uniform. He was walking fast and headed right in our direction. Within a few moments, when he looked up from what he was reading, my heart skipped a beat, and I knew who it was. It was Marc!

"Mom, is that Marc?" I asked.

"Yes, Lori, it is. Dad has already arranged for him to have a four-hour pass so the two of you can visit, and we are here to pick him up. He will be with us in a few moments," she told me.

I was in shock! I had no idea what might happen next. What would I say to him? How should I act? How did Dad manage to get him a four-hour pass? Why hadn't I figured out where they were taking me?

When Dad returned to the car, Marc was walking right behind him. Mom moved over to the middle of the back seat, and I sat by the window. Marc climbed into the seat next to Mom and said hi to everyone.

I looked at him, and our eyes met briefly, and my head began to spin. Mom and Marc were already having a conversation. All I was getting from him was a glance now and then.

My attempt to understand what was taking place at that moment is with me to this very day. All I knew was that I wanted to leap over Mom, hug Marc, and tell him I was glad to see him, but my body just sat there, in a daze, not moving!

Dad then drove us to a nearby park, pulled over, and stopped the car. Mom said to Marc and me, "Okay, you two, this is where you get reacquainted with each other."

With that, she asked Dad to open the car's trunk. She pulled out a blanket, handed it to Marc, and told him to take me for a walk.

Marc took the blanket from Mom, took my hand, and said, "Come on, Lori, let's find a place so we can visit each other."

We walked for a few minutes, and he stopped near the edge of a beautiful lake, a reasonable distance from Dad's car. He found a spot and spread out the blanket.

He stretched out and laid back on the blanket. I sat at the far corner at his feet and took a deep breath. What was he going to say to me? How am I going to handle this? For someone who liked to talk, I was suddenly speechless!

For a few moments, we just sat there and looked at each other. Then Marc started talking. "Lori, your mom told me that you are engaged to someone. Have you forgotten that I gave you a cigar engagement ring long ago and asked you to marry me, and you said yes?" he asked.

"Marc, of course I remember that, but it has been a few years since I've heard from you or even knew if you were alive! You've always been in my heart. I always wondered why you never answered any of my letters. Not hearing from you told me you no longer cared for me."

Marc then told me, "I found out that my mom always got to the letters you wrote to me before I did, so I didn't get any of your letters, and since I never heard from you, I felt you no longer cared for me. But I want you to know that you stayed in my heart, and I have never forgotten you. Do you think we can start over? Will you break off your engagement, so you and I can plan for our future? I'll arrange to come and see you as soon as my training is over in a few weeks. We need to spend time together. I truly care for you and want this to work."

At that moment, I knew my life would change and be what I had always wanted it to be. Marc then glanced over his shoulder and saw that Dad's car was still within sight, so he got up, pulled me to my feet, folded the blanket, and asked me to come with him.

I would have gone anywhere he wanted me to at that time, but I had no idea where he was taking me. He had my hand, and I could feel the warmth coming from his body—the warmth I hadn't felt in a long, long time!

He led us behind a large concrete wall close by, where he knew no one could see us, then took me in his arms. He gently tilted my chin to touch his and told me he had always wanted to kiss me but had always respected me too much.

That sweet kiss was the one I had waited for for so many years. My tears would not stop flowing after it ended. I couldn't hold my emotions any longer. Marc just held me tight for what seemed forever while I continued crying. Then in a few moments, he spoke in my ear, "I love you, Lori. I always have, and I always will."

We stood there for quite some time, just holding each other. We didn't need to talk; words weren't needed between us. We both knew what we felt was love.

The walk back to Dad's car and then the drive back to Lackland Air Force Base seemed to last only a few moments. I didn't want it to end, and I didn't want to let go of Marc's hand. Marc looked at Mom and told her that he would be coming to see us in a few weeks and that he was so grateful that she had called him. Then he winked at Mom and told her, "Lori and I have some plans to work out."

He hugged me tight, not wanting to let go. With that, he walked out of my life again, but I knew it would be different this time.

CHAPTER 44

Breakup with Robert, 1954

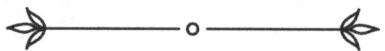

It was dark and cloudy on our way home, just like my mind. I went over and over in my head what had just taken place.

I kept asking myself, Did that all just happen? Did Marc tell me that he had always loved me and thought I had forgotten him? After not seeing or hearing from him for almost two years, did he think I didn't care for him? Had his mother kept my letters from reaching him? Did he honestly want to come and see me when he got out of training? So many questions were spinning in my head. All I knew was when he climbed into the back seat of our car next to Mom, my heart was his.

Marc never talked much, so I felt those words coming from his mouth while looking at me with those dark eyes were sincere. Before, they had been words I had only heard in my dreams. But this time, they came from him.

The engagement ring around my neck had to go back to Robert. That would be the first thing I needed to do. He was off to camp with the Navy for a few more weeks, so I would have to wait until he returned. I wasn't looking forward to doing what was needed, but I had no choice.

Mom asked me if I was okay and how I felt about Marc after seeing him. All I could tell her was that I was so glad she and Granny had made that call and that they were both right in knowing Marc was the only one I had always loved.

It was two weeks before Robert was back in town, and when he called, I told him I needed to see him. That afternoon I drove to his home and had a lovely welcome from his parents and sister.

They told me he was in the backyard and for me to go on out there and surprise him. Robert was surprised because I hadn't told him I was coming over. He grabbed me and hugged me so tight it was hard to breathe.

"Lori, I missed you so much!" he said.

He had my hands in his and instantly noticed no ring was on my finger. His look was one that I will never forget.

"Robert, I have had time to think about us getting married, and I know it is the wrong thing. I don't want to hurt you, but I know my heart. Please know I care for you as a dear, sweet friend, but I can't go further than that with our relationship," I told him. Then I took the ring I had in my pocket and placed it in his hands.

After a few moments, he turned, walked away, and said nothing. I knew nothing else I could say to him would help, so I went back into the house and walked out the front door back to my car.

His parents and sister didn't even notice that I was leaving. By the time I reached my car, Robert was outside on his knees on their sidewalk with a hammer hitting what I knew was the ring. He just kept on smashing it over and over. Tears came to my eyes as I drove away. Hurting someone is not an easy thing to do.

I was so glad Granny was still living with us. She was someone I knew I could talk to and always share my feelings with. I told her what I had done, and she assured me I did the right thing by returning the ring to Robert. "Lori, you need always to follow your heart. And we all know that your heart has always been with Marc," she told me.

She was right about that; I know Granny had always liked Marc. When I told her that he said he was coming to see me, she was excited.

My first letter from Marc came within eight days. I was almost afraid to open it, still unsure about his true feelings. Even having a short note from him was a surprise, as writing a letter to me had never been something he took seriously.

Tears of pure joy flooded my cheeks as I read and re-read his letter. He repeatedly told me how much he loved me and that he could hardly wait until we could see each other again, and that he wanted me to start planning for us to get married. Oh, how many years I had waited to hear those words! The joy I was feeling was almost unreal.

CHAPTER 45

Making a Tough Decision

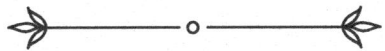

I t was the middle of July 1955, and my senior year at school would start soon. I had paid twenty-five dollars as a down payment for my senior ring and needed to turn in another twenty-five dollars to get it before the school year started.

I asked Dad if he would help me with that cost, and his answer was no. If I wanted a ring, I should pay for it myself. He also told me that I would no longer have that fantastic car I loved so much, as he had lost it at one of his gambling parties, and the new owner was going to pick it up in a few days.

The things that Dad did never really surprised me. I learned the hard way a long time ago that I could not trust or depend on him for anything.

Now that I was going to marry Marc and move to Tulsa, I decided I shouldn't have to worry about school. And not having a car anymore didn't bother me a lot, either. Those things were no longer necessary to me. I needed to concentrate on making as much money as possible to help pay for our wedding.

My decision not to return to school was difficult for Mom and Granny to accept. I needed to help them understand that since I would be getting married and moving away to Tulsa in the middle of the school year, it made no sense for me to continue.

My boss at the Dairy Queen put me on a full-day work schedule when he found out I was not going back to school, so I was pleased about that. I could save money and stay busy to help the time pass quicker, and he also gave me a small pay raise.

Waiting to see Marc again seemed to take forever. I received my second letter from him just a few days after the first one, and he told me he would go home before coming to see me. He wanted to go home to get a few basic clothes, a swimsuit, and his car, and then he would drive down and spend a week with me. He also repeated how much he had always loved me and could hardly wait to hold me in his arms again.

My boss at the Dairy Queen knew what was going on in my life and was happy for me. When I told him that Marc was coming to visit, he told me I could take that week off to spend time with him and not worry about being at work.

I was glad to hear that! My work buddies and boss were dear to me and helped me keep busy. In the evening, some of the ones I worked with would go to a show with me, and, when possible, we would run out to the beach to have fun and just pass the time. They all knew my story about Marc and were very supportive.

Marc called me a few days later and told me he was headed to Texas and couldn't wait to see me. It was about a ten-hour drive, and I spent those ten hours just looking out our kitchen window, waiting for his car to drive up.

After all these years, since I was ten and he was twelve, could this be happening? I remembered the time he and I climbed that tree when I lived in Tulsa, and he had carved a heart on a limb and put our initials in the center. I remembered many times when we would get close and my family would move again, and I would lose my friendship with him. Could this time be for real? Would I move away again, but this time move with him?

When Marc made it to Texas, our week of being together was so wonderful. We laughed and talked and hugged and kissed so many times. Marc was so gentle and careful with me all the time. Not once did he try to go beyond the hugging and kissing. We had so much fun at the beach and wherever we went. We were together, so that was all we needed.

Mom and Granny planned a trip for us to see the Battleship of Texas and have a picnic together. While there, Granny asked Marc if he would walk with her so she could talk to him without me being around. I caught the wink Granny gave me, so I knew whatever she had on her mind would be okay. She loved Marc and was very happy to have him there with us. I watched as they walked away, Marc had his arm around her, and I was so glad to see how much they liked each other. I found out later that what she wanted to talk to him about was me not finishing school.

The next evening when we were back home alone, Marc talked to me about our plans for our future. "Lori, you know that I love you very much and want us to get married as soon as possible," he said, "but I also want you to know that I want to be able to take care of you. I want to get a good job, save a little money, and have a place to live before getting married. I don't know how long that will take, but I want you to understand I'll make it happen as fast as possible and assure you that we will work things out if you remain mine and stay patient with me."

"Marc, I'll wait until you are ready, as long as I know that someday soon we will get married and be together," I answered.

"I promise, Lori, I'll do everything I can to make it happen. It may take a little while, so why don't you go ahead and finish school until then?" he asked me.

"I'll think about it, Marc, but I don't want to return right now. I'm happy working and enjoying the friends I have at work. I know I should go back, but not right now," I told him.

His promise to me when he said that he was working hard to get us together was all I needed. I had waited for years, so I could surely wait a few more months.

Marc was with me a few more days before he had to return home. As I watched him drive off that morning to return to Tulsa, my heart again went with him, but I knew he would work hard to get a job and make me his wife.

He did get a job after just a few weeks. He went to work as an apprentice electrician and also decided to join the union. His dad told him that would be the best thing he could do if he wanted to make decent money. Marc loved and trusted his dad and listened to him for advice.

I knew I had to take each day as it came and do the best I could to stay busy. Time passed faster as long as I kept busy and tried not to count the days. My job and the evenings I spent with friends just going to the beach or a show helped.

I also found out that going to church with Granny on Sundays helped fill the weekends. She had joined a Methodist church within walking distance from where we lived and always took me, the twins, and Terrell with her. Mom was usually at work, and Granny never asked Dad to take us, so we always walked.

I loved the church and the preacher and decided that would be where Marc and I would get married. Granny wanted all of us to know God better than we did, so she did all she could to help us learn. One night, instead of my Granny reading the Bible to all of us, she asked me to start reading it to the twins and Terrell before bedtime.

Granny was always in the room with us, but I did the reading. We all learned things together about the Bible, and I enjoyed being the older sister to my younger siblings. It made me feel special!

One of the chapters I read one night was about forgiving others. Could I ever forgive my dad for the past? I knew that I should, but could I? I had buried those past years deep and had not discussed them with anyone, not even Marc. I never took a chance to be alone around Dad, and he never came close to me for attention after we had moved to Texas. I felt he was also keeping the past buried. Could I forgive him, as I knew I should, according to what the Bible said?

CHAPTER 46

Ellen's Wedding: Okmulgee, 1956

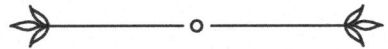

Granny had been with us for almost a year when she got a letter from my aunt Sue, who lived in Okmulgee. Ellen, her daughter and my favorite cousin, was getting married in May, and Ellen wanted Granny to be at her wedding.

Aunt Sue also mentioned that Ellen wanted me to be a bridesmaid at her wedding. Aunt Sue asked Granny if she could come back home and bring me with her.

After we talked to Mom about this, she agreed that we both should make the trip to Okmulgee to be a part of Ellen's wedding. Mom also decided that it was time that Granny moved back to Okmulgee and lived in the little house that Uncle Chuck had built for her.

In May, Mom arranged for us to ride a bus to Okmulgee. I also asked my boss if I could be off work for at least two weeks, and he agreed.

I didn't want to write a letter to Marc, so I called him and told him I was coming to Okmulgee and that he might also be part of Ellen's wedding. It had been three months since we had last seen each other, so he was as happy as I was about getting together again.

The bus trip was awkward, but being with Granny made it fun. She always had a fun side to life, and I loved her for it. When we made it to Okmulgee, Aunt Sue, Uncle Chuck, and Ellen met us at the bus station with loving hugs and open arms.

It was good to be with a family that loved each other so much. Ellen was even more beautiful than I remembered, and the glow she had told me she was happy. Later that evening, Granny told me to go ahead and call Marc and let him know we were here and find out when he could come to see us.

Marc was waiting to hear from me and told me he would drive down early the following day and spend the day with me. He also told me that he would be with me as much as possible while I was there. Once again, we were going to be together. His love was still with me, and I felt loved when I was with him.

The next day when Marc arrived, we went for a short drive together, and I noticed he was quieter than usual, so I knew he had something on his mind. He told me that his dad had become sick with cancer, had to quit work, and was home. Marc loved his dad very much and knew he had to do his part in helping his mom and dad in any way he could. That meant he needed to help them with expenses since his dad's income had stopped.

"Lori, I know that I want to be your husband, and I want us to be married. Please understand that since Dad is so ill, he may not live very long, and I have to do all I can to help them," he told me.

I could sense the pain in Marc's voice and his sadness. I knew I needed to help support the weight he was carrying. What else could happen to interrupt our marriage? When would our time come? It had been almost a year since we knew we wanted to be married, but things kept happening to stop it.

Marc did tell me that he had been looking at rings, and hopefully, the next time we would see each other, he would be able to place one on my finger. I asked him if it would be okay if we got married in a Methodist church, and the smile on his face was all I needed to see.

"Lori, I didn't know you went to a Methodist church. I joined our Methodist church last month and have been going every Sunday!" he told me.

We both looked at each other with disbelief as neither of us had ever talked about what church we attended.

"To get married at your Methodist church is perfect. I hope we can do it soon. Let's push for some time this coming January!" he said.

"Oh, Marc, that will be wonderful. I'll keep it small and start making a few plans. Let's see how Ellen's wedding goes, and maybe we can get some ideas."

Ellen's wedding was beautiful, and the long, flowing, light-blue bridesmaid dress she had me wear made me feel beautiful. Marc told me I was stunning, and coming from him, it made me feel pretty. Ellen had also asked Marc if he would be an usher during her wedding, and he told her he would be honored to help in any way.

After the wedding, while we were all at the reception, Marc asked me if I thought I could spend one day in Tulsa with him before I had to return to Texas. He wanted to take me to a jewelry store to show him what type of ring I wanted. He had looked at many different ones and found it too hard to choose. He couldn't make up his mind. He would feel better if I could show him what I liked.

I talked to Aunt Sue since she was who I was staying with, and she said yes, I could spend a day with him in Tulsa, and she thought it would be good for us to go together to pick out our rings. Marc then arranged with his mom for me to stay with them for one night.

It didn't take me long to pack an overnight bag. It would mean one more day I could spend with Marc and even pick out a ring that he would soon place on my finger.

Marc promised Aunt Sue and Uncle Chuck that he would have me back late the following day. They both agreed and also let me know that since Granny was going to stay in Okmulgee, they didn't want me to ride a bus all the way back to Texas by myself, so they arranged for me to return home with my aunt Louise and uncle David, who had also come to the wedding. They lived in Pasadena, Texas, within an hour's drive from where I lived, and Mom could drive there and get me. I liked that idea better than riding back on a bus by myself. It was fun with Granny, but I was unsure how it would be by myself.

The day I spent with Marc's mom was hard for me. I never cared for her much since I knew for a fact that she always threw away the letters that I would write to him, and she was the main reason he could not come and see me during the summer when we were both in school together because she didn't like what my dad did for a living. But I kept it as pleasant as possible while I was with her.

I loved talking to his dad, who was very ill in a hospital bed in the middle of their front room. He was an easy person to love. While Marc was at work, I did all I could to stay out of the way and be kind to both. Once Mr. Lucus asked me to come closer to him so he could talk to me as I walked through the room.

"Lori," he said, "I know you and my son are going to get married soon, and I want you to know that Marc has talked to me about you since you were both in grade school. I want you to know that he loves you and wants nothing more than to have you with him. All I ask of you is for you to take care of my boy and love him back."

He took my hand in his sad, weak hand and kissed it. It was all I could do to keep the tears away, as it was evident that he was pretty ill.

Marc got off work at five, and as soon as he came home and changed clothes, he and I headed to the jewelry store. It didn't take me long to show him the ring set I liked the best. He agreed and put them on layaway right then. A few months' payments would be all it would take, and he could have them ready to be ours.

"Lori, if we can hang on a little while longer, we'll make this marriage happen. I'm so tired of waiting. I want you now," he said to me.

His gentle hug and kiss right there in front of the person who waited on us at the jewelry store made me feel very loved.

On our drive back to Okmulgee, I was almost sitting in his lap while he was driving. I wanted to be as close to him as possible because I knew we would be apart again for a few more months. It was now May 1956, and we both had agreed that January 1957 would be our wedding month. That was going to be another long eight months. But Marc felt that would be how long he would need to have things in place before he took me as his wife.

"Lori, I'm so lucky to have you. You are so patient with me, and I know it's hard for you. I love you very much, and you're always in my thoughts. I'll do all I can to speed things up. Please understand I have to feel like I can take care of you and give you what you deserve," he told me.

"I know, Marc, but you better promise me right now that you'll write to me more often! I can't stand it when I don't hear from you for weeks at a time," I told him.

"I know, I'm terrible about that, but I'll try harder. Just know that you are always with me in my thoughts," he said.

Aunt Sue and Granny were waiting for us when we drove up in the driveway, and it was already late in the evening, so they were beginning to worry. Marc told them he was sorry but had to take me to a jewelry store to help choose our wedding rings.

Granny looked at Marc and told him it was about time! She also told him he better hurry things up, as she wanted to be alive to see us marry. Marc hugged her tight and told her he was working hard to make it happen faster. I could see their love for each other, which was a wonderful feeling.

I walked with Marc as he was going to his car to leave. *One more time*, I kept telling myself. Hopefully, this being apart would end soon. I knew he would be gone again with one more hug and kiss.

"I love you, Marc," I said.

"WHY?" was his answer.

"You know why, Marc. Don't be silly."

"Why?" was his reply again.

"Because you love me back!"

"Why?" he said again with that silly grin!

"Oh, Marc, stop it!" I told him as I hit him on the arm.

With his silly grin, he backed out of the drive, waved out the window, and was once more gone!

CHAPTER 47

Planning Our Wedding, 1956

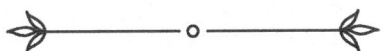

I was very grateful that Aunt Sue and Uncle Chuck had arranged my trip back to Texas with Uncle David and Aunt Louise instead of on a bus. Uncle David was my mom's older brother, and I liked my Aunt Lousie. They were both fun, and our trip back to Texas was good. I was going to miss Granny, but she was back in her tiny home in Okmulgee now and was happy.

Mom came and got me, and I was happy to see her. On our drive back home, I told her that Marc and I were planning on January to get married. I also told her he had joined a Methodist church, so he was happy to hear that we would get married in one.

"Mom, it will be nine more months before then, so we will have to work out another trip to see each other again," I told her.

"Lori, I'm sure we will be able to work out something for you. That is a long time to be apart. It reminds me of the time I wanted to see your dad when he was in the service and was gone so long. Trust me; it strengthens your love for each other," she said.

I was glad to get back to work at the Dairy Queen and be with close friends. They kept me busy in the evenings. I think we saw every movie that came out and knew every seagull on the beach.

One of the girls I worked with had become a very close friend, and I asked her if she would consider being my maid of honor at my wedding. Sidney was her name, and she was excited to do that. I talked to her about the colors I wanted to use in our wedding, and she loved the choices I had made. Since it was going to be wintertime, my idea was to have a dark green and light green color for the girls, and I wanted them all to be velveteen.

I also loved the idea of red and white poinsettia flowers all over the church as decorations. I talked to Mom about the twins, who were now nine years old, and Terrell. I wanted them all to be a part of our wedding.

I wanted Lousie to be my flower girl dressed in a cute velveteen green dress, and I wanted Lee to be the ring bearer. He could wear a green cummerbund of velveteen and a tie. Terrell could be an usher and also wear a green velveteen cummerbund. Mom agreed and said it would be fun putting it all together, and we could have a small reception at home after the wedding with cake and punch.

"You still need to decide on the type of music you want and who you might get to sing," she said.

"I'll talk to Marc, Mom, and see what song he might like to hear," I told her.

I struggled with the decision of having Dad be the one to walk me down the aisle. He would not be a part of my wedding if I had my way. But if I chose to keep him out of it, people would ask too many questions. I didn't want to have that burden, nor did I want Mom to deal with it.

Once again, I had to put my ugly past with my dad deep down in my memory. I knew with Marc standing at the end of the aisle smiling at me, anyone could be walking me down that aisle.

Marc had a birthday in June, and I wanted to be with him to celebrate so bad. He would be twenty years old. I was unsure what to get him, so I called to ask him. It was faster than writing a letter, and I needed to hear his voice anyway.

"Lori, you don't need to get me anything. Just put your money in the bank to help pay for the next trip you'll make to Tulsa," he said.

"Well, Marc, what makes you think I'll be making the next trip?" I asked.

He then told me he had just started a new job that would pay well and knew it would be best not to take a week off.

"Your boss at the Dairy Queen lets you off when you ask for it, so I think you'll have to be the one to come here instead of me going there," he told me.

"Okay, Marc, you're right. I hate that I can't be with you on your birthday," I replied.

"Well, yours is in July, and I want to be with you. We both know the time will come when we can share those days and be together," he said.

"How's your dad, Marc?" I asked.

"He's not doing well at all, Lori. The doctors have told us he might only have a few more weeks," he told me.

I could feel the pain in his voice, and I wanted so much to be able to hug him. "I love you, Marc, and I'll say a prayer for him tonight," I told him.

"I love you too, Lori, and will count the days until I see you again," he said.

Since Granny decided to stay in Okmulgee when we made our trip for Ellen's wedding, Mom decided it was time to quit work. She decided it was time to stay home and take care of the twins and Terrell. I was glad she stopped working because work was getting hard on her, and she was never in a good mood when she came home. It was time for her to quit!

I wasn't sure if Mom was tired or did not feel good. When Dad got home in the evening, all they seemed to do was argue. I missed Granny so much. She was my rock most of the time. I promised her I would continue attending church and reading the Bible, so I made it a point to have mom drive me, the twins, and Terrell to the church every Sunday. I wanted her to go inside with us for the service, but she never would, and neither would Dad. So I just took charge and did what I had promised Granny I would do.

My eighteenth birthday came in July, and I received a beautiful sweater in the mail from Marc, along with a sweet phone call. Marc said he loved his new job, and it was paying well, and now that he was in the union, he knew that his pay would increase. He had also been working hard on getting a decent car that would make the trip to Texas without him worrying about it breaking down. He told me he had bought a 1955 Chevrolet in great shape. "The only change I want is to paint it and put new pipes on," he told me.

"Just don't make it a stock car, Marc," I said.

He laughed at me and promised me he wouldn't do that. "I wish I could be there with you, Lori, for your birthday," he told me.

"I know, Marc, and thank you for the beautiful sweater. Mom will take a picture of me, and I'll send it to you in my following letter. And by the way, is your arm broken? I haven't received a letter from you for over two weeks."

"I'm sorry, Lori, I think about it during the day, but once I get home and help Mom with Dad, I just forget," he said.

"Please remember, Marc. I hate it when people ask me how you are, and I can't tell them," I told him.

"I'll try to do better, Lori, but remember you're always with me in my thoughts. I just don't write them all down," he answered.

"Well, you better start writing them down, or I may forget to write to you! If you do nothing more than sign an X and put it in the mail to me, at least I've heard from you!" I told him.

"Okay, Lori, I'm sorry, and I'll try hard to do better. I love you, and happy birthday again," he said.

Within a week, I did receive a letter from him in the mail! I was happy to know he had taken me seriously about writing more often and could not wait to see what he had to say. I wanted to know how his dad was and if he liked his new job.

When I opened the envelope, I found a big X in the middle of the letter, and a "Love, Marc" signed at the bottom. That was it—nothing else! I had asked for it, and he did what I'd told him. After I got over the shock, I had to laugh! It was funny.

It felt like forever before August came, and I planned my next trip to Tulsa to be with Marc for a few days. The letters were better after that silly X, but I needed to feel his arms around me and to be able to look into those dark eyes.

I had no choice but to ride the bus to Tulsa and make it fun. Mom took me to the bus station and gave me many last-minute instructions. I found a seat by the window and was doing fine until a young man sat beside me and started talking. At first, I was a little uncomfortable, but I soon realized he would be okay. However, I kept my guard up as Mom had told me.

The bus trip was long, and it didn't get into Tulsa until after dark. I was thrilled that Marc was standing just outside the steps that led out of the bus to greet me with a big hug! It didn't take long to get my bag and head to his car, where we could be alone.

"Lori, I thought that bus would never get here! Did you do okay; did you have any problems?" he asked me.

"No, Marc, I did fine. A very nice young man sat beside me and kept me company," I told him.

"I bet he did," was his reply.

I laughed at him and said, "Well, hurry up and marry me so you won't have to worry about another fella!"

He smiled and kissed me again and said, "Five more months and I will make that happen."

Mom had arranged for me to stay with Aunt Beth and Uncle Doug while I was in Tulsa. That was great as far as I was concerned, as I didn't want to stay at Marc's home. Since it was already late at night, Marc took me straight to Uncle Doug's.

They only lived about twenty minutes from where Marc lived, which made it better for Marc. He liked my aunt and uncle and was glad I would stay there. It was a Friday evening and he didn't have to work weekends, so we had the whole weekend to be together.

After a short visit with my aunt and uncle, Marc hugged me and said he would see me around ten in the morning. Uncle Doug said he would love to take us to the park for a picnic on Sunday afternoon after church if that would be okay, and of course we both agreed.

Saturday, we spent some time with Marc's mom and dad and then rode around and visited some of Marc's friends. We made our wedding plans, and he liked my chosen songs.

We agreed on "The Lord's Prayer," "Because," and "Oh Perfect Love." I told him our singer was my friend and would not charge us. He was happy with the plans that I had made and said he sure hoped that some of his family would be there.

"Just have your mom give me names and addresses, and I'll send them an invitation. I'm sure they will be there if they can," I told him.

Going to church with Marc was special. The Methodist church in Tulsa that he went to was massive! We sat upstairs in the balcony, and I couldn't get over how big it was. Of course, everything in Tulsa was big, and I just needed to remember that since it would be where I would live in a few months.

The picnic at the park was fun, too. It had a zoo that we went to, and then we roasted some weenies and marshmallows. My time with Marc was always a happy time. He always made me feel special when I was with him.

"Lori, would you like to go to the drive-in tonight?" he asked me that day. "There is a movie I want to see, and I think you will enjoy it."

"That will be fun, Marc. Just let me go back to the house to change clothes and let Aunt Beth know I'll get in late. What is the name of the movie?" I asked him.

"*From Here to Eternity* is the name, and it will be a special one for you to see," he told me.

Marc visited with Aunt Beth and Uncle Doug while I changed clothes and got ready to go.

"I'll be a little late, Aunt Beth, but I'll be quiet, so I won't wake you," I told her.

"Don't worry, Lori, I may be up anyway, as I don't go to bed early," she said.

"Okay, I'll see you if you're still awake," I said.

It had been a long time since I had been to a drive-in, and Marc assured me I would like the movie, so I was ready for a fun evening. The film was good, and I was enjoying it, but in the middle of it, Marc reached out the window, turned the volume down on the speaker, pulled me close to him, and gave me a very long kiss.

"Do you remember what the name of this movie is, Lori?" he asked me.

"Yes, Marc, you said it's called *From Here to Eternity*," I said.

The smile I saw on his face, even in the darkness of the car, told me something was going on. Then he reached across me into the glove box, pulled out a small package, and opened it.

"With this ring I am placing on your finger, I want you to know that my love for you and our marriage will be 'from here to eternity,'" he said softly.

As he slid my engagement ring on my left hand, I was in shock, and soon the tears were flowing. "Oh Marc, you had this all planned, didn't you?" I said.

"Well, I guess you could say so. Will you be my wife?" he asked me.

After I gained my composure, I looked at him and said teasingly. "Well, let me think about it!"

I saw a few tears in his eyes at that moment, but they were tears from laughter. We had both waited and wanted this moment for so long. It was finally here, in the darkness of the night and in the middle of the movie *From Here to Eternity*, a beautiful film and one I'll never forget!

CHAPTER 48

A Special Christmas, 1956

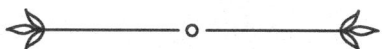

A few days later, Marc put me on the bus to return to Texas. It got more challenging every time we had to part, but we knew this time it would only be for five months because our wedding would be in January.

I was excited to show off my ring to Mom and my friends when I returned home. And I knew it was time to start getting my dress made and to get serious about our wedding plans. I needed to start sending invitations as soon as Mrs. Lucus sent me the addresses for Marc's side of the family. I had never met them, so I hoped they could come.

I received a letter from Marc within a week of being home, and it wasn't one that I was glad to get. He told me that his dad had passed away. He told me that he knew his dad was a Christian and loved God. He knew his dad was no longer in pain and was with someone that loved him.

"I only wish that you had been here with me, Lori. I would like to have had you standing by my side at his funeral. Dad made all his arrangements for his burial. He had taken care of everything. Mom and I didn't have to worry about anything. I only hope I can be half the man he was when my time comes," he told me.

I was sad that I wasn't able to be there for Marc. Just knowing he wanted me with him was painful. I was so glad I had taken the time when I was there to talk to his dad. And when I saw him, he had asked me again to take care of his son! I promised him for the second time that I would do everything possible to make Marc behave himself, and when I said that, I saw a sweet grin on his dad's sad face.

My best girlfriend Sidney and some of Mom's close neighbor friends started making arrangements for a bridal shower. Everyone got busy with dresses and the decorations that we would need.

Five months would pass quickly, and we didn't want to rush into making plans at the last minute. It had been a month since Mr. Lucus had died when Marc called me and asked me how I would feel about changing our wedding to December instead of January.

He told me that his mom had decided she wanted to move to California to be close to others in her family and start a new life. She had told him that we could live in her house, and she would only charge us a small rental fee. He also said his new boss told him he could have a week off during Christmas if I wanted to schedule it.

"My gosh, Marc, that's a lot to take in. How do you feel about all of it?" I asked him.

"I love it, Lori, if it's alright with you. That means we can be married sooner," he said.

"Marc, let me talk to Mom and make sure we can have the church earlier. I'm glad I haven't mailed out the invitations or written down our wedding date. I don't want to do it on Christmas, but maybe a few days ahead. I'll call you back as soon as I find out what day the church will be available," I told him.

"Okay, I'll be waiting to hear from you! I love you very much," he said.

I couldn't wait to talk to Mom about our conversation, but first, I called the church and talked to our pastor. He told me the only day they would have would be December 23rd. That just happened to be Mom's birthday, so I wasn't sure how she would feel about that.

"Lori, I think that would be wonderful! Let's put it on the calendar now!" she told me.

I also checked with Peggy, our singer, and my maid of honor, Sidney. The date change worked for them, so I called Marc and told him December 23rd at five o'clock p.m. was when we could get married.

I then asked him when he was planning to drive down.

"Let me schedule it from December 21st until January 1st. That way, we can spend Christmas with your family, then head back to Tulsa on the 26th. That will give us time to settle in before I return to work. We can have a short honeymoon night somewhere in Houston. Will that work for you?" he asked me.

"Yes, it sounds beautiful to me! I'll get the invitations out with the date and get things started. I'm so ready," I told him.

"Me too, Lori. Me too!"

That wonderful day, December 23rd, was finally here, and my heart was full of love. I spent a few hours with Marc before he had to spend the night with Wayne, his best man. That was one of the rules Wayne told us. When you get married, the groom cannot see the bride the night before the wedding.

Marc had wanted his favorite cousin Lee to follow him down in his car and be his best man, but Lee couldn't make it, so at the last moment, he chose my dad's best friend, Wayne. Marc said he was okay with that since Wayne was in the car when this all started back at Lackland Air Force Base.

It made me sad to know that none of Marc's family would be at our wedding or be there for him. They all lived in different states, and being close to Christmas made it more difficult for them to be away from their homes.

Marc and I accepted it and understood. They had all sent us beautiful gifts and money, so we felt loved. It was a small wedding but, to me, a beautiful wedding. The red and white poinsettias and the green velveteen dresses were perfect.

As I stood in my white velveteen wedding dress, just outside the door leading into where Marc was standing at the end of the aisle, he was all I could see. I knew others were there, but Marc was all I saw. Peggy was singing "Oh Perfect Love," and I had to fight the tears. I then took Dad's arm, and he walked me down the aisle to give me to Marc.

Those gorgeous dark eyes were smiling at me, then he reached and took my hand. All those years and months suddenly disappeared, and I could hear my granny's voice telling me, "Maybe Tomorrow!"

I wanted to shout out loud and tell her as I said "I do": "My 'tomorrow' is here, and it is beautiful! After all those long years of being apart yet always loving each other, we are married, and I'm now Mrs. Marc Lucus! Life is just now beginning, and it will be wonderful."

I had no idea what lay ahead for the two of us. I only knew that we had a love that was so very strong that I felt like we could handle anything that might come our way. We both had God on our side, and with Him, all things are possible.